AN INTRODUCTION
TO THE FOUNDATIONS
OF LUTHERAN EDUCATION

AN INTRODUCTION TO THE FOUNDATIONS OF LUTHERAN EDUCATION

WILLIAM C. RIETSCHEL

Concordia Academic Press
A Division of
Concordia Publishing House
Saint Louis, Missouri

Copyright © 2000 Concordia Academic Press
3558 S. Jefferson Avenue, Saint Louis, MO 63118-3968
Manufactured in the United States of America

Library of Congress Cataloging-in-Publication Data

Rietschel, William C.
    An introduction to the foundations of Lutheran education / by William C. Rietschel
        p.   cm.
    Includes bibliographical references.
    ISBN 0-570-04286-0
    1. Lutheran Church—Education—Philosophy. I. Title.
LC574 .R56   2001
371.017'41—dc21   00-010074

1 2 3 4 5 6 7 8 9 10   09 08 07 06 05 04 03 02 01 00

CONTENTS

PREFACE

An Introduction to the Foundations of Lutheran Education is an overview of the foundations of Lutheran schooling in the United States. It developed from my teaching "Perspectives of the Teaching Profession" and "Foundations and Ethics of American Education," two preservice undergraduate courses designed to introduce prospective teachers at Concordia University, River Forest, Illinois, to nonpublic and public school teaching in American society. These are similar to "Introduction to Education," "Introduction to the Foundations of Education," and "Introduction to Educational Policy Studies" courses offered in colleges and universities throughout the country. Over a period of more than two decades of teaching these courses, I experimented with various organizational schemes and all of them presented weaknesses. However, the greatest deficiency was the unavailability of a parallel text that would place Lutheran schooling into the larger social context that was being explored.

This book is written for students who are preparing for the teaching ministry in The Lutheran Church—Missouri Synod (including those enrolled in teacher colloquy programs) as well as for those who simply wish to learn more about key concepts regarding, and issues and policies affecting, Lutheran schooling in America. Because of the target audience and also because the text attempts to tell the story of Missouri Synod schooling, I have utilized synodical publications as source material whenever they were available so that external interpretative influences might be minimized. While I welcome external lenses and believe the Missouri Synod might benefit from more analysis by outsiders, I wanted as much as possible for the Synod to speak for itself. How successful I was remains for the reader to determine. Ultimately, however, it is my lens that bears responsibility for the selection and interpretation of the sources and is also accountable for the pages that follow.

The text consists of nine chapters preceded by an introduction that considers factors in choosing to become a servant in a Lutheran school classroom. The ensuing two initial chapters provide an historical context by examining the events and ideas that have contributed to the development of formal educational endeavors within the Synod in the United States.

The philosophical foundations of Lutheran education are examined in chapters 3 and 4 through an exploration of the theoretical, philosophical, and theological underpinnings to what Neil Postman in his trenchant book, *The End of Education*, has called "a transcendent spiritual idea that gives purpose and clarity to learning."[1] In a very real sense, these two chapters are the cornerstone of this excursion into the foundations of Lutheran schooling. It is my ultimate hope that this junket will direct the reader's mind to a narrative "that tells of origins and envisions a future, a story that constructs ideals, prescribes rules of conduct, provides a source of authority, and, above all, gives a sense of continuity and purpose" for the present and the future of Lutheran schools.[2]

The next two chapters explore the place of the teacher within the ministerium of The Lutheran Church—Missouri Synod and such factors and issues as supply and demand, preparation and certification requirements (including teacher colloquy), placement procedures, satisfaction with the teaching ministry, and stress, burnout, and attrition.

Chapters 7 and 8 present an overview of the organization, governance, administration, and financing of Lutheran elementary and secondary education and the legal forces that impact them.

The final chapter attempts to provide a glimpse of the present and a vision for the future ministry of the Lutheran school. Change may require risk and it is natural for one to resist it. Consequently, one needs to move more positively toward change buoyed by Paul's words, "If anyone is in Christ, he is a new creation; the old has gone, the new has come" (2 Corinthians 5:17).

It needs to be pointed out that I have resisted the temptation to try to include everything. To do so in an introductory book tends to confuse the important with the temporary and to make the treatment current but superficial. What appears in the subsequent portions of this book is my attempt to create a knowledge base, a stable core, that introduces prospective teachers to Lutheran schooling in the United States.

This undertaking would not have been possible without the contributions, feedback, and support of a number of individuals. To Robert Toepper, professor of education at Concordia University, River Forest, who wrote and contributed chapter 5, I extend my deepest appreciation. His work aptly represents his knowledge and long-standing commitment to the preparation of teaching ministers for The Lutheran Church—Missouri Synod. To Dwayne Mau, former staff executive for education of the Atlantic District, The Lutheran Church—Missouri Synod, and current pastor of St. Paul Lutheran Church, Monroe, New York, I tender profound gratitude for his efforts toward and contribution of chapter 9. His visionary leadership has influenced many regarding the church's ministries and he has personally helped me to examine and expand my ministry paradigms. I would also like to thank the following individuals who reviewed this book: William Preuss (Concordia University, Seward), Donald Sellke (Concordia University, St. Paul), and Lawrence Sohn (Concordia University Wisconsin).

---

[1] Neil Postman, *The End of Education: Redefining the Value of School* (New York: Alfred A. Knopf, 1995), 5.

[2] Postman, *The End of Education*, 5-6.

They made useful suggestions and provided thoughtful reactions in the development of the manuscript. Their conscientious contributions to the text are sincerely valued. I also wish to note my gratitude to my mentor, Gerald Gutek, professor emeritus at Loyola University, Chicago, ever gentle, yet the consummate scholar. Thanks also must be extended to my editor, Dale Griffin, at Concordia Academic Press. Finally, I give special thanks to my wife, Shari, who genially prods me to work toward excellence in all things, and our three daughters, Michelle, Lisa, and Kimberly, who continually remind me that I'm still learning. My love of teaching is exceeded only by my love for them. And it is to my children that this endeavor is dedicated. Just as this text attempts to tell the great, transcendent story of synodical schooling, by God's good grace and favor it is they who will ultimately continue and tell my story, however small a blip it might be within the context of God's kingdom here on earth. To him be the glory!

William C. Rietschel
Concordia University
River Forest, Illinois

INTRODUCTION

WHY TEACH IN A
LUTHERAN SCHOOL?

When the author enrolled in college, one of his relatives questioned him about his interest in becoming a Lutheran teacher. "Why don't you pick a career in law, where you get a lot of prestige and are able to make a big salary?"

I resented the tone of the question, but must admit that I did not do a particularly good job of answering it because I had not seriously pondered my motives for Lutheran teaching. Anyone who is thinking about becoming a Lutheran teacher should examine his or her motives for wanting to become one and also should understand something about the situation of Lutheran schooling and the Lutheran teaching ministry. The subsequent chapters will examine that footing. We begin, however, with a fundamental issue: Why teach in a Lutheran school? Your reasons for choosing Lutheran teaching will undoubtedly affect your attitude and behavior toward your students. Whatever these reasons may be, it will be helpful for you to consider the thoughts and feelings that have motivated others to teach in Lutheran schools. Listen to their voices.

> The Lutheran school allows me to help the cross touch the lives of children in a most personal way. Both the law and the gospel can be seen in the cross, and it is that word that can be demonstrated and communicated.[1]

> The song "I love to tell the story of unseen things above, Of Jesus and His glory, of Jesus and His love ..." answers the question, "Why teach in Lutheran schools?" Teaching the story of God's love enriches and fulfills the lives of children, their families, and the teacher involved... . Teachers in Lutheran schools are privileged daily to express that love of Christ with children, their families, congregation members, community, and partners in church ministry. They teach it in Bible stories, in all subjects throughout the day, on the playground, at lunch, in giving and receiving loving touches during the day, in the smile that says "You're someone very special—I love you," in discipline that lovingly corrects wrong, in the giving and accepting of forgiveness, in the caring, in challenging and helping children to become what God created them to be, in being a "little Christ" to others. ...

---

[1] George Guidera, "Why Teach in Lutheran Schools?" *Lutheran Education* 119 (May-June 1984), 241.

Having Christ's presence, His love, and His commission to communicate this love with His help, the Lutheran teacher is truly blessed. This is the joyful life![2]

Why teach in Lutheran schools? Why not? What a grand blessing to be on a "co-mission" with Jesus Christ, assisting in the care of souls in a manner consistent with the Word of Christ.[3]

Inherent in a response to the question, "Why teach in Lutheran schools?" is the obvious rationale: "to serve the Lord of the church through Christian education." (This is, of course, not to say that individuals who teach in other educational systems fail to serve their Lord, but rather it indicates the peculiar nature of "sacrificial giving" demonstrated by Lutheran school teachers and administrators.)

It is ... necessary to contemplate a single significant factor of the question under consideration. In few professional realms would a worker experience the unique fulfillment that is to be encountered in Lutheran education among Lutheran ministers—a fulfillment generated by the people of which the staff is composed. ... [T]hey collectively exemplify the concept of the Body of Christ. Anchored by the Word, unified by the Sacraments, and supporting the ministry with prayer, the parochial school staff enjoys a unity in a single-minded goal—service!

Lutheran educators ... challenge life with love, sincerity, purpose, and peace. And their motivational impetus emanates from the vertical dimension of grace (what God gives to man) with the resulting horizontal dimension of response (how man deals with man). ...

Why teach in a Lutheran school? To experience the blessings of the unique interpersonal relationships that are God's gift to his servants.[4]

Why teach in Lutheran schools? ... [P]ublic and private school counterparts experience many of the same joys as teachers in Lutheran schools. All ... watch children progress throughout their educational lives. We who are involved in Lutheran Christian education have a thrill which they cannot share, however. That is watching the power of the Holy Spirit at work in the lives of these people. We feel an even greater thrill when they lead their parents to the same altar to profess their faith. Lutheran teachers who are privileged to remain in one school long enough will find former pupils enrolling

[2] Robert Hentscher, "Why Teach In Lutheran Schools?" *Lutheran Education* 119 (May-June 1984), 242.

[3] Doris E. Hrachovina, "Why Teach in Lutheran Schools?" *Lutheran Education* 119 (May-June 1984), 243.

[4] Steven A. Allmon, "Why Teach in Lutheran Schools?" *Lutheran Education* 119 (September-October 1983), 1.

their sons and daughters because they want their children to experience and know the same love, guidance, and direction which they received.

Why teach in Lutheran schools? To follow God's call to proclaim the Good news of Jesus Christ. Teaching is a tremendous way to be of service to people. God may use our guidance and example so that, by the power of the Holy Spirit, they may be led to a stronger faith in Jesus Christ.[5]

Why teach in a Lutheran school? Because not only is it a joyous experience to see children grow as total people in Christ, but also because I know that it is a calling which my Lord holds in the highest esteem. For as we feed His lambs, we are in turn fed generously from His loving and bountiful hand.[6]

Lutheran teachers ... are no more intelligent or wise than their public school counterparts. However, they do have one bit of wisdom which adds an extra dimension to all they do. That wisdom is the Word of God and the dimension it adds is the freedom and power to teach within the circle of Christ's arms. In the words of St. Paul, "I *know* whom I have believed . ..."

Why teach in Lutheran schools? Simply because of Christ, whose promises are eternal. That makes work a pleasure.[7]

I am a Lutheran teacher because God has called me to be one.[8]

Thus people who choose to become Lutheran teachers are led by a variety of motives. Those who are thinking of entering the teaching ministry—and even those already in service—need to ask themselves why they are making the choice. Motives may include a love of children, a desire to impart knowledge, an interest in and excitement about teaching, or a desire to perform a valuable service to society. But most importantly, teaching in a Lutheran school is a unique call to serve God's people. Because God first loved, Lutheran teachers now love others. They are choosing, in a sense, to express their love for God and people through the ministry of teaching. They are being called by God and being asked to make a commitment to service. It is hoped that an exploration of the ensuing pages will assist the reader in hearing the call and making the commitment.

---

[5] Richard H. Blatt, "Why Teach in Lutheran Schools?" *Lutheran Education* 119 (September-October 1983), 2.

[6] Robert E. Marty, "Why Teach in Lutheran Schools" *Lutheran Education* 119 (November-December 1983), 62.

[7] Jeanine Meyer, "Why Teach in Lutheran Schools?" *Lutheran Education* 119 (January-February 1984), 121.

[8] Eunice Merz, "Why Teach in Lutheran Schools?" *Lutheran Education* 119 (March-April), 182.

1

EUROPEAN ANTECEDENTS
OF LUTHERAN EDUCATION

Why should the reader of this text care about the ancestral shaping of ideas regarding Lutheran schooling? What difference does it make? The history of Lutheran education, the focus of this and the subsequent chapter, offers insight and perspective for the prospective Lutheran schoolteacher. Just as the study of American history can contribute to the loyalty and appreciation a citizen of our country may have, so the knowledge of Lutheran educational history can build loyalty and commitment to the teaching ministry.

To be sure, preservice Lutheran educators should avoid anchoring themselves securely in the safety of completed events. However, many of the problems of Lutheran education have grown out of the past and are intimately connected with it. In order to understand contemporary issues in Lutheran schooling, the student preparing for a ministry in teaching must be aware of how they developed.

Interpreting our educational past is never finished because it affects our sense of self and our power to influence the course of future events. Lutheran teachers must think in terms of the future in order to prepare those they serve to cope with whatever events and issues may develop to affect them. To do so, those preparing for the Lutheran teaching ministry need to understand the history of Lutheran educational ideas and develop a collective educational memory. Having done so, they will better appreciate the distinctively Lutheran contribution to the transmission of the larger cultural heritage and better be able to examine and reassess Lutheran educational and cultural traditions as a guide for making judgments about the future.

In a very real sense whoever controls the interpretation of the past—the beliefs about Lutheran education's origins—gains an immense power in interpreting the present and perhaps shaping the future. Without a knowledge of our educational heritage and its meaning, prospective Lutheran teachers are, in effect, disempowered.

Finally, the history of Lutheran education may serve to recall past techniques and concepts with which those who have previously served in the teaching ministry have had success or failure. Much of what is regarded as new or innovative in education generally has a long historical record. Lutheran education should not overlook these experiments, for they can supply valuable information on proposed educational change. Simply, without a knowledge of the past, Lutheran teachers may find themselves "reinventing the wheel." Given the ever-shrinking availability of financial resources, this would not be good stewardship.

This chapter and the next cannot possibly include all the historical influences on Lutheran education. However, by providing an overview of the past, they attempt to empower the preservice Lutheran teacher to understand the present and build the future.

BACKGROUND FACTORS OF THE PROTESTANT REFORMATION

When on October 31, 1517, Martin Luther posted his ninety-five theses on the door of the Castle Church at Wittenberg, he set in motion a religious revolution challenging the authority of the Catholic Church. His "justification by faith alone" challenged the traditional Catholic doctrine of salvation and good works. Luther's ideas spread, resulting in a reformation among both Protestant and Catholic Christians. Martin Luther became the focal point of the religious Reformation; the resulting turmoil immeasurably benefited education.

The Reformation's religious ferment occurred against a backdrop of political and economic change in Europe. Among the background factors contributing to the Protestant Reformation were the following:

1. *Individualism.* The spirit of individualism that was awakened during the Renaissance sought to defend the rights of the individual against the encroachment of institutions. The extension of this attitude to the individual's religious rights occurred during the Reformation period.

2. *Spirit of Criticism.* The criticism of religious abuses went unheeded by the Vatican. During the Renaissance, secular and religious critics found fault with traditional Roman Catholic doctrine, ritual, interpretation of the Scriptures, and conduct of the clergy.

3. *Secularism.* The growth of secular feeling during the Renaissance provided a fertile field for the growth of hostile feelings toward religious institutions.

4. *Religious Abuses.* The widespread immorality during the Renaissance in Italy affected the church. Religious leaders frequently led lives as corrupt as any in the secular world. Luxury and sensuality invaded a papacy very much in need of reform. Priests, entrusted with solicitation of funds for a new and more impressive St. Peter's Church, frequently abused the doctrine of religious indulgences, selling those indulgences for money.

5. *Rise of Secular Political Power.* Perhaps the single most important factor in the success of the Protestant Reformation was the assistance it received from secular political authority. The princes of Germany and the monarchy of England benefited from a limitation of papal power. Monasteries that were tax-free owned rich lands, which employed hundreds of farmers. Large sums of money, exacted from the countries of Europe, went to the enrichment of the papal court. The seizing of church lands and the reduction of revenue that could be sent to the Vatican served to check Vatican power and to increase the wealth and authority of the rulers of western European countries, particularly those of Germany and of England.

6. *Popular Unrest.* While many princes and aristocrats were affluent during the sixteenth century, the common people suffered economically. The impoverished commoner seemed doomed to a life of periodic unemployment, inferior education, and heavy taxation. Church taxes and church abuses led many common people to hold attitudes receptive to Protestant teachings.

7. *The Printing Press.* With the invention of movable type in 1450 and the refinement of paper, Protestant doctrine could be spread with great rapidity. Henry VIII was able to demand the use of the same textbooks in every school in England. Thanks to the printing press, the translation of the Bible by Luther could be distributed throughout Germany. Since this translation was in the vernacular, large numbers of people could read it with understanding.

PRINCIPLES OF THE
PROTESTANT REFORMATION AFFECTING EDUCATION

The above setting and historical background of the Protestant Reformation bring into further focus the educational principles and changes that it subsequently fostered. The balance of this chapter will provide an overview of the main principles stemming from the Protestant Reformation. These views affected education and the views on education held by Luther, Bugenhagen, Melanchthon, and Sturm.

Three principles affecting education emanate from the religious Reformation initiated by Luther and the other reformers. The first of these was that the authority of the Bible was substituted for that of the church. Going back to the beginning of the Middle Ages and up until the days of the Reformation, the final authority in matters of faith and life was the church. Therefore, it was not necessary that individual members of the church themselves be able to explore and to search out the truths regarding their own religious convictions. They were in effect told what to believe. However, all of this changed when the final authority in matters of faith and life was given to the Bible. Now it would no longer do to tell the people what the church said. To be guided by the authority of Scripture, the people themselves needed to know the Bible. Therefore it now was necessary to convey what Scripture says.

A second principle affecting education resulted from the religious principle that the judgment of the individual, rather than that of a church council, priest, or church tribunal, was to be normative or decisive for a person in one's interpretation of Scripture. Luther's impassioned words at the Diet of Worms are reflective: "Unless I am convicted by Scripture and plain reason ... I cannot and I will not recant."[1]

A third principle affecting educational change brought about by the Protestant Reformation was that the final responsibility for the salvation of individuals rested with them rather than upon an institution, that might intercede for them. The sale of indulgences, the prepayment of masses for the living and the dead, and other abuses had placed final responsibility for salvation upon an institution. The reformers removed this responsibility, and the burden for salvation was placed on individuals rather than on an institution.

One of the effects of these three principles was the necessity for the common person to be able to read the Bible in his or her own language. Luther produced the first complete and popular Bible translated from the Hebrew and Greek. Instruction in the vernacular became essential as a part of the Protestant Reformation. Those affected by the Protestant Reformation began to feel responsible for informing themselves regarding the teachings of the Bible.

The assertion by Protestant reformers such as Luther that people should read the Bible in their own language required an extraordinary effort to create a literate populace. The Protestant Reformation was a powerful force in extending primary schooling to larger sections of the population. A range of authorities such as the various churches, the towns, or the districts founded primary schools. Vernacular schools were primary institutions that offered a basic curriculum of reading, writing, arithmetic, and religion.

The Protestant reformers ultimately contributed to the rise of universal schooling. Germany led the way in organizing a state educational system, that provided free compulsory elementary education for every boy and girl.

The educational changes brought about by the Protestant Reformation did not evolve independently. There was a good deal of propagandizing, structuring, and planning involved. Luther, as well as others, provided leadership in effecting these changes.

MARTIN LUTHER

Schools in Germany, and to an extent throughout Europe, had fallen upon difficult times. Economic changes made useless much that medieval-minded

---

[1] Roland H. Bainton, *Here I Stand: A Life of Martin Luther* (New York: New American Library, 1960), 144.

schools had to offer. Political change had increased the desire of civil authorities to control education within their particular realms. When monasteries and cloisters were closed in Lutheran lands, their schools died. Cathedral and other church schools disappeared. German reading and writing schools, as well as Latin grammar schools, were undersubscribed.

Martin Luther was deeply distressed by the state of the schools. He recognized the necessity for schools in any society, especially in one making a transition between two cultures. He once said that if he were not a priest, he would be a teacher. At another time he affirmed that even if there were no heaven or hell, schools still would be necessary for life on this earth.

Luther's contribution to the educational reform of his day consisted of writing, preaching, and organizing. He wrote two pamphlets, or open letters. The first was "To the Christian Nobility of the German Nation Concerning the Reform of the Christian Estate," written in 1520. In 1524 Luther wrote the second pamphlet, or open letter, "To the Councilmen of All Cities in Germany That They Establish and Maintain Christian Schools." In 1530 Luther preached "A Sermon on Keeping Children in School." Finally, when he wrote his Small Catechism, he included a preface that encouraged the study of the chief parts of Christian doctrine.

As Luther studied social conditions in Germany, he was appalled by the ignorance, immorality, impiety, and delinquency that he found almost everywhere. It seemed to him that the people, freed from paternal supervision, were unable to live in freedom with responsibility. He pointed up an important phase of this responsibility in "A Sermon on Keeping Children in School," in which he emphasized the necessity of education for both the religious and the secular life.

It was necessary to encourage the people to send their children to school. Under the old regime of the Middle Ages the necessity for reading and writing was, so far as religion was concerned, minimal. Under the principles of the Reformation everyone needed to be able to read the Scriptures. In his sermon on sending children to school Luther pointed out to the parents that they were withholding from the state and from the church the gifts that God had given them in the form of future pastors, teachers, statesmen, and civil servants. If they refused to send the children to school, God would hold them accountable for their negligence. In this way he tried to get the state and the church to combine in the promotion of education for the common people.

Luther's strategy was simple, logical, and effective. In order to reform the educational program in Germany, it was necessary that people with the authority to erect and maintain schools be alerted to the common benefits gained by an educated citizenship. In his address "To the Christian Nobility of the German Nation Concerning the Reform of the Christian Estate," Luther urged princes and civil rulers to establish elementary schools in which all children could be taught religion, languages, history, singing, instrumental music, and mathematics. In his letter "To the Councilmen of All Cities in Germany That They Establish and Maintain Christian Schools," Luther stated,

> My dear sirs, if we have to spend such large sums every year on guns, roads, bridges, dams, and countless similar items to insure the temporal peace and prosperity of a city, why should not much more be devoted to the poor neglected youth—at least enough to engage one or two competent men to teach school?[2]

In this way he encouraged and stimulated action on the part of the cities of Germany to establish schools and employ teachers to train children.

Luther not only translated the Bible from the original languages into the language of the common people, i.e., German, and thus initiated the effort to provide the Scriptures in the vernacular throughout the world, but he also provided the Small Catechism. This was to be the Bible for the masses, supplemented by Aesop's fables, in which he found many moral principles interestingly illustrated. Luther prefaced his catechism with this rationale:

> The deplorable destitution, which I recently observed, during a visitation of the churches, has impelled and constrained me to prepare this Catechism of Christian Doctrine in such a small and simple form. Alas, what manifold misery I beheld! The common people, especially in the villages, know nothing at all of Christian doctrine; and many pastors are quite unfit and incompetent to teach. Yet all are called Christians, have been baptized, and enjoy the use of the Sacraments, although they know neither the Lord's Prayer, nor the Creed, nor the Ten Commandments, and live like poor brutes and irrational swine. Still they have, now that the Gospel has come, learned to abuse all liberty in a masterly manner.
>
> O ye bishops! [H]ow will ye ever render account to Christ for having so shamefully neglected the people, and having never for a moment exercised your office! May the judgment not overtake you![3]

Also contained in the preface are insights into Luther's view of instructional methodology. For example, he believed that the teacher of the catechism should not expect to accomplish too much in one lesson. Rather, the teacher should take a comparatively small section such as one commandment and explain it as thoroughly as possible. Then this should be reviewed before going on to the next lesson. Luther also pointed out the advantage of using the same text with children when it came to the truths of God's Word.

Luther believed that every boy and girl should receive a free elementary education. "Today," he wrote, "we are living in a different world, and all things are

---

[2] Theodore G. Tappert, ed., *Selected Writings of Martin Luther: 1523–1526* (Philadelphia: Fortress Press, 1967), 42.

[3] Martin Luther, *Small Catechism* (St. Louis: Concordia Publishing House, 1912), 3–4.

being done differently. My idea is to have the boys attend such a school for one or two hours during the day, and spend the remainder of the time working at home, learning a trade, or doing whatever is expected of them." Luther believed that boys spent "at least ten times as much time anyway with their pea shooters, ballplaying, racing, and tussling." And "[i]n like manner, a girl can surely find time to attend school for an hour a day, and still take care of her duties at home. She spends much more time than that anyway in sleeping, dancing, and playing." However, Luther believed that "the exceptional pupils, who give promise of becoming skilled teachers, preachers, or holders of other ecclesiastical positions, should be allowed to continue in school longer."[4] They should go to the Latin grammar school, which the town established and supported. There they would study Latin, Greek, and Hebrew, the Scriptures and church fathers, history, and music.

Luther believed that only those young men who completed the education offered by the Latin grammar school and who demonstrated intellectual ability ought to be given the opportunity to attend a university. There they would study the Scriptures and become bishops and priests or prepare for public service. Luther did not approve of higher education, i.e., the Latin grammar school or university, for women. A woman's place was in the home. The purpose of women was to bear as many children as possible.

Luther placed ultimate responsibility for education on the state. The state should have concern about education because the educational system would mold the individual who would defend and support the government. Because of the responsibility of the state in education, Luther held that among its obligations the state should

1. provide the financial support of every school,

2. ensure the attendance of every child by passing compulsory education laws, and

3. supervise the curriculum, books, and teaching in the schools.

In sum, Luther came to realize that the use of freedom required maturity of understanding that few had. He believed that education was the only avenue to maturity. He gave the world a faith that set human beings free and thinking, a philosophy of education that opened new vistas, and a vernacular Bible. As an influential figure in history, he changed Europe and set patterns in education, state, and church that were to determine much of the future.

Three educators, each with unique talents and specialized abilities, contributed to the development of Luther's ideas in the schools of Germany. These were Johannes Bugenhagen, Philip Melanchthon, and Johann Sturm. Under their guidance, town schools were reformed, princes reorganized or established

---

[4] Tappert, *Selected Writings of Martin Luther*, 62-63.

schools in line with Protestant thinking, and Germany was well on its way to incorporating much of Luther's thinking into its educational structure.

JOHANNES BUGENHAGEN

Bugenhagen was entrusted with the establishment of Lutheran schools in northern Germany. If princes and other civil rulers were to build and operate schools in accord with Lutheran thinking, it was necessary that they have guidance and direction. This Bugenhagen gave. He drew elaborate plans for school systems in a number of cities and princely realms. For each he planned an entire educational system, from reading and writing schools through Latin grammar schools. He also made provisions for libraries and a form of adult education. Some historians have credited him with being the father of the *Volksschule* (or the elementary people's school).

His success in building elementary schools throughout the area brought him to the attention of the king of Denmark. He received a commission to organize Lutheran elementary schools in Denmark, where towns had maintained reading and writing schools under control of the church long before the Reformation. Bugenhagen insisted that they be transferred to municipal control, that teachers be appointed by civil authorities, and that although parents would support them through fees, teachers would receive extra compensation for teaching church music, religion, and the catechism. Under this plan, the traditional town school with a faculty of clerics came under the control of the civil government and served as an instrument for developing loyal Protestants.

Above these reading and writing schools in Bugenhagen's school ordinances, and decidedly superior to them in Protestant thinking, were Latin grammar schools. These were also under civil control and taught the classics and religion.

Like Luther and most of the reformers, Bugenhagen believed that education should be available to both boys and girls. Therefore, in every plan he drew, there were separate schools for each sex.

PHILIP MELANCHTHON

Melanchthon was a lifelong friend of Luther. That friendship ended with Luther's death in 1546. After Melanchthon's death, Melanchthon's body was laid to rest alongside Luther's at the University of Wittenberg. Melanchthon, a Greek scholar and a university professor, was a master teacher who knew how to make difficult ideas and concepts understandable to his students. He received his master's degree at the age of seventeen. Realizing the inadequacy of the textbooks then in use, he wrote a Greek grammar when he was sixteen. This book went through forty-three editions over the next one hundred years. Later he wrote a Latin grammar, destined to be in use for over two hundred years. During his lifetime, Melanchthon published 709 works, exclusive of his letters. Among these diverse publications were works in psychology, religion, history, ethics, physics, rhetoric, and logic.

Melanchthon, like Luther, "rejected the virtual monopoly that the medieval church had enjoyed over the schools and the licensing of teachers" and also "looked to the state to exercise these functions."[5] Like Bugenhagen, Melanchthon served as an educational counselor to princes and authorities. In this role he participated in many school surveys and had a hand in preparing several school codes. However, his most significant contribution to the development of state-controlled education in Germany was in 1527 when he wrote the *Book of Visitation*, the first school survey ever written. This resulted in the Saxon Code, a school plan for Saxony written by Melanchthon and revised and edited by Luther. This code set a pattern for much Protestant educational thinking.

The Saxon Code recommended a three-level organization of school classes. The first level should study German, basic Latin, reading, and writing. Religion and morality should hold an important place in teaching. Each reading should have some moral lesson for the young boys and girls. This level of education, comprising three classes, developed into the *Volksschule*, compulsory for all German children. Although Melanchthon made no recommendation about the number of years to be spent at this or subsequent levels, six years came to be allotted to each level in the centuries to come.

Secondly, there were to be Latin grammar schools for the more able children. This level became the modern *Gymnasium* of German education. Grammar, dialectics, and rhetoric in both Greek and Latin were to be studied. Melanchthon recommended this curriculum to protect and defend the new faith. In keeping with the thought of the humanists of his day, Melanchthon claimed that classical studies provided the means by which the student could assimilate the ideas inherent in the Greek and Latin writings.

Finally, the universities of the state were to be the capstone of the system. Here the students were to prepare to serve the church and the state in the professions of religion, law, medicine, or teaching.[6]

Melanchthon held teaching in the highest regard. A teacher was viewed as a protector of truth and justice who served both church and state. Although teachers were paid very little in Reformation Germany, the status of teachers became higher. The prestige enjoyed by European teachers in subsequent ages may be attributed in part to the efforts of Melanchthon.

Melanchthon's work in education actively continued until his death. The *Volksschule*, *Gymnasium*, and several universities came into being through his

---

[5] Gerald L. Gutek, *A History of the Western Educational Experience* (2nd ed.; Prospect Heights, Ill.: Waveland Press, 1995), 141.

[6] Ellwood P. Cubberly, *The History of Education* (Boston: Houghton Mifflin, 1920), 316-317.

efforts. A year before his death in 1560, the first system of education made its appearance in the Duchy of Wurttemburg. A century later, all of Germany was organized into this three-tiered pattern of education.

JOHANN STURM

While Sturm shares with Melanchthon the honor of being a founder of the *Gymnasium*, or secondary school, of Germany, Melanchthon's secondary program of studies soon yielded to that of Sturm. He, too, was a product of the University of Wittenberg. He founded his school at Strasbourg, and it soon became the best known secondary school in Europe. Its course of study was transported to America, where traces can still be discerned in some liberal arts colleges.

The plan Sturm submitted to the Strasbourg town authorities, and which eventually was adopted by them, proposed a *Gymnasium* of ten classes or grades, each with its own teacher. Boys were accepted at the age of five or six.

Sturm had a clear conception of what a school should do and worked this into a plan of studies and a curriculum that was specific and detailed. In good humanist tradition, he believed that Latin was the essence of learning. The educated man was the cultured man. This man must know and know that he knows. He must be a master of pure and elegant diction and use Latin skillfully, and he must be religious. Religion, Greek and Latin, and logic were the basic subjects of his curriculum. All these should produce the "cultured man," one who could use Cicero's Latin with eloquence.

The one exception to Sturm's exclusive emphasis upon speaking and reading Latin in the schools came at the beginning of the educational cycle, when the child was permitted to memorize the Lutheran catechism in the vernacular. Later the child was required to translate this catechism into Latin. This was followed by reading St. Paul's writings in Greek and then translating them into Ciceronian Latin. Instruction in religion was given only on weekends, with the exception that psalms in both Latin and Greek were sung each morning.

Sturm prepared a detailed syllabus for each class, stating what should be taught each day and the proper method of teaching it. He left nothing to chance or the teacher's discretion. The school was a lockstep institution; all boys moved along at the same pace under the same techniques. Sturm wrote texts for some of the classes, discussed his method and curriculum with educators and other interested persons who came to see him from all parts of Europe, corresponded widely on educational matters, and never tired of proclaiming Latin, as Cicero wrote and spoke it, the true mark of an educated man.

Sturm's *Gymnasium* became popular in a short period of time in England as the Great Public School. In the Scandinavian countries it continued to be known as the *Gymnasium*, but its scope was reduced slightly and mathematics, modern languages, and natural sciences were introduced.

The *Gymnasium* became the preparatory school for five or six more years in a college or university. Because it took the child into this intensive classics program at a very early age, it was possible for those who survived the rather rigorous program of studies to graduate at age fifteen or sixteen. The college or university, in turn, became what today would be regarded in the United States as a graduate school.

MISSOURI'S EDUCATIONAL ROOTS IN GERMANY

Since the Protestant Reformation was fundamentally religious, it was natural that religion would become the major interest of the schools. The Bible in Latin or Greek was part of the curriculum of German schools. Further, since Lutheran polity influenced church reorganization, pastors were required to teach the catechism and give religious instruction to all children. Often reading and writing were added to these pastoral schools. When the pastor found himself too busy to care for this responsibility, he either employed a teacher who became part of the church's staff or turned the work over to the sexton or sacristan. In time, examinations were set up for teachers in these church schools, supervised by municipal officials. Often, acting as representatives of the municipality, it was Lutheran pastors who inspected the religious curriculum and examined the teachers employed in the school.

Missouri Synod Lutheran education in America has its roots in Saxony. It was in 1838 that an exodus from Germany began under the leadership of a pastor from Dresden named Martin Stephan. The cause of the exodus was primarily religious. Stephan had united a dissent against the established church of Saxony. This dissent swam against the strong current of rationalism that the Enlightenment had sent streaming into all aspects of German culture. These Saxon Lutherans viewed this rationalism as dangerous. This apprehension coupled with the encouraged amalgamation of German and Reformed congregations would blur the distinctive features of their Lutheran heritage.

While not a factor in the exodus, it is helpful to understand that because the Saxon Lutheran pastors frequently acted as representatives of the state regarding parish schools, the battle over rationalism was joined often at the level of the parish schools. The supervisory authority of the pastor was neither arbitrary nor final. He was responsible to the crown's Ministry of Worship and Public Instruction. The dissenting Lutheran pastors who tried to correct perceived rationalism in the school's instructional program were at risk of being reported to those above them in authority. They were often reprimanded.

Summing Up

It was the antecedent of the dissent of the Protestant Reformation that made Germany education conscious. It was the antecedent of dissent against rationalism that initiated the historical development of Lutheran education in America. It is to the latter narrative that we turn in the next chapter.

Discussion Topics and Suggested Projects

1. Critique the author's rationale for why a prospective Lutheran teacher should have some knowledge of Lutheran educational history.

2. The author provides a brief overview of the forces influencing educational changes brought about by the Protestant Reformation. What forces are influencing contemporary Lutheran schooling?

3. Read Luther's "To the Christian Nobility of the German Nation Concerning the Reform of the Christian Estate," "To the Councilmen of All Cities in Germany That They Establish and Maintain Christian Schools," or "A Sermon on Keeping Children in School." Prepare a paper and/or presentation that illustrates the key ideas of the assigned selection.

4. Is it correct to assert that the Protestant Reformation is the hinge upon which modern American public education turns? To broaden your perspective in answering this question, explore John Calvin's influence on colonial New England education and the subsequent common school movement.

5. The Protestant Reformation was influential far beyond Germany and also triggered the Catholic Counter-Reformation. A number of popular secular texts in the historical foundations of western education also treat such educational reformers as Roger Ascham, John Calvin, Sir Thomas Elyot, Ignatius Loyola, Richard De Montaigne, and Peter Ramus among others as significant contributors to changes in education. Prepare a brief biographical description for each, exploring their major ideas on learning, instruction, and the purposes of schools, and what their impact might be on educational practices today. Organize a panel to role-play these theorists together with those considered in this chapter.

6. Imagine yourself twenty or thirty years from now—as a Lutheran educational theorist and reformer. What are your major ideas on teaching, learning, and Lutheran schools? To help with your essay, think about your strongest educational beliefs and the aspects of Lutheran education that you would most like to change. Be as "revolutionary" as you like, but try to provide supporting reasons for your ideas.

Resources, Influences, and Suggested Further Reading

Bainton, Roland H. *Here I Stand: A Life of Martin Luther*. New York: New American Library, 1960.

Cubberly, Ellwood P. *The History of Education*. Boston: Houghton Mifflin, 1920.

Gutek, Gerald L. *A History of the Western Educational Experience*. 2nd ed. Prospect Heights, Ill.: Waveland Press, 1995.

Luther, Martin. *Large Catechism*. Philadelphia: Fortress Press, 1959.

_____. *Small Catechism*. St. Louis: Concordia Publishing House, 1912.

Painter, F. V. N. *Luther on Education*. St. Louis: Concordia Publishing House, 1928.

Spitz, Lewis W., and Barbara Sher Tinsley. *Johann Sturm on Education*. St. Louis: Concordia Publishing House, 1995.

Tappert, Theodore G., ed. *Selected Writings of Martin Luther: 1517-1520*. Philadelphia: Fortress Press, 1967.

_____. *Selected Writings of Martin Luther: 1523-1526*. Philadelphia: Fortress Press, 1967.

_____. *Selected Writings of Martin Luther: 1529-1546*. Philadelphia: Fortress Press, 1967.

2

HISTORICAL DEVELOPMENT OF LUTHERAN EDUCATION IN AMERICA

This chapter builds on the previous one in attempting to provide an overview of the historical influences on contemporary Lutheran education in America. Among old-church Protestants in the United States, Lutherans have long been active in maintaining schools. Interestingly, however, the actual number of schools maintained by the largest Lutheran body, the Evangelical Lutheran Church in America (ELCA), has remained relatively small. For example, in 1998–1999 ELCA had 233 elementary schools and 14 high schools. By contrast, the significantly smaller Wisconsin Evangelical Lutheran Synod maintained 366 elementary schools and 23 high schools during the same period.[1]

Historically, the most enduring story of Lutheran school activity has remained that of The Lutheran Church—Missouri Synod. For two reasons the schools of the Missouri Synod, especially parish elementary schools, will be the principal focus of the subsequent pages. First, this text is directed primarily toward a Missouri Synod audience. Second, compared to other Lutheran bodies, the Missouri Synod possesses the greatest numbers, 994 elementary schools coupled with 68 high schools.[2] For a teacher in the Synod's schools to appreciate their purpose, one does well to understand their historical development in America.

In telling the narrative of the considerable activity in establishing and maintaining schools, one may point to two distinct waves. The initial wave began with the colonial period. The second occurred during this country's early development as a nation.

COLONIAL BEGINNINGS AND EARLY NATIONHOOD

The original colonial Lutherans consisted of the Swedish, Dutch, and German settlements in the Middle Atlantic colonies, primarily in Pennsylvania.

---

[1] Ross E. Stueber, ed., "1998-99 Statistical Report Summary, Schools and Early Childhood Centers of The Lutheran Church—Missouri Synod" (St. Louis: Department of School Ministry, The Lutheran Church—Missouri Synod, 1999), 11.

[2] Stueber, ed., "1998-99 Statistical Report Summary, Schools and Early Childhood Centers of The Lutheran Church—Missouri Synod."

Lutherans could also be found in small clusters scattered through Virginia, the Carolinas, and Georgia.

The first Lutheran school established in the colonies, probably in the present state of Delaware in 1640, was Swedish. There is evidence that when the Salzburg Lutherans from Austria settled in Georgia in 1734, they established schools as well as congregations in Georgia and some in the Carolinas. Eighteenth century German immigrants and the "father of American Lutheranism," Henry Melchior Muhlenberg, who arrived in Pennsylvania in 1742, organized a significant number of churches and schools. In 1752, St. Matthew, Manhattan, the oldest Lutheran school still operating today, was founded. Thus, at the onset of the nineteenth century, thriving Lutheran schools of Scandinavian, German, and Dutch origin could be found in the following states: New York, New Jersey, Delaware, Pennsylvania, Maryland, Virginia, North and South Carolina, and Georgia. Walter Beck speculates that during the period from 1640 to 1820 the total number of Lutheran schools established may have been in excess of 400.[3]

The second wave of Lutheran schools began about 1820, just as the initial eastern wave was declining. This subsequent wave concentrated itself in the central and north central states and was a direct consequence of the flow of religious dissidents from Germany and Scandinavia who came to the United States seeking religious freedom and economic opportunity.

These immigrants wanted to perpetuate their language and culture. Thus they also gathered in clusters, but this time further west, scattered over the plains, villages, and forest clearings and along the rivers of what are now Ohio, Michigan, Indiana, Illinois, Wisconsin, Minnesota, and Missouri. It was there that they established congregations, schools, colleges, seminaries, foreign language newspapers, publishing houses, and other social and cultural agencies. The new immigrants were joined by migrants from the Middle Atlantic states, many of whom were Lutheran. It was not uncommon in these settlements to find a Lutheran parochial school, housed in a log cabin, serving Lutheran and non-Lutheran children alike. These early Lutheran schools would teach a common branch curriculum, i.e., reading, writing, and arithmetic, in the mother tongue with some instruction in English for good measure. For example, St. Lorenz Lutheran School, established in 1846 in the farming community of Frankenmuth, Michigan, was a pioneer school serving Native American children, the offspring of Bavarian missionaries, and the children from the newly settled farms in the area. It is from such modest beginnings that the school system of The Lutheran Church—Missouri Synod grew.

---

[3] Walter H. Beck, *Lutheran Elementary Schools in the United States: A History of the Development of Parochial Schools and Synodical Educational Policies and Programs* (St. Louis: Concordia Publishing House, 1939), 47.

FORGING SYNODICAL SCHOOLS

In a sense, the Missouri Synod opened its first school when Martin Stephan and his group of Saxon dissenters set sail from Germany in 1838. Their emigration code stated that "during the voyage the children shall receive necessary instruction."[4]

Be that as it may, upon arrival in St. Louis in 1839, these same Germans rented a two-story house for the purpose of conducting school. The area constituting the first floor was set aside for church meetings and for classroom use and also had a section in which a teacher could live. The second level of the house served as a parsonage.[5] When the majority of the group left St. Louis for Perry County, Missouri, work began on a "college" modeled after the *Gymnasium* they had known in Germany. The faculty was made up of four ministers, each a university graduate. In point of fact, the school in which all instruction took place was neither a college nor a secondary school, but only a one-room cabin with eight male students and three female students in attendance. Their ages ranged from five to fifteen years.

By the mid-1840s the Saxons in Missouri had drawn closer to several other Midwestern congregations. Each seeking a more conservative affiliation, twelve charter congregations met in Chicago in 1847 and formed the German Evangelical Lutheran Synod of Missouri, Ohio, and Other States (the original name of The Lutheran Church—Missouri Synod).

SOWING AND SPREADING SYNODICAL SCHOOLS

The twenty-five year period following the formation of the new synod was one of successfully sowing and spreading Lutheran schools. By 1872 the Synod had grown from the original 12 charter congregations to 446 and the number of schools from 14 to 472.[6] Enrollment exceeded 30,000 students.[7] Two factors contributed to this early success.

First, the Synod's strategy was to have a Lutheran school in every congregation. The usual scenario was the simultaneous establishment of a congregation and school. Occasionally, a school was built prior to the establishment of the parish. The premise for all of this activity was that the founders of the Missouri Synod generally considered Lutheran schools to be "a self-evident and simple necessity. [I]n their constitution ... no congregation or parish could become a member of Synod unless it maintained a school for its children."[8]

---

[4] Walter O. Forster, *Zion on the Mississippi* (St. Louis: Concordia Publishing House, 1953), 574.

[5] August C. Stellhorn, *Schools of The Lutheran Church—Missouri Synod* (St. Louis: Concordia Publishing House, 1963), 82-83.

[6] Stellhorn, *Schools of The Lutheran Church—Missouri Synod*, 94-97.

[7] Stellhorn, *Schools of The Lutheran Church—Missouri Synod*, 171.

[8] Stellhorn, *Schools of The Lutheran Church—Missouri Synod*, 66.

The second factor contributing to the early success in sowing and spreading Missouri's schools was the model provided by Melanchthon's Saxon code coupled with the ideas of Johann Sturm that were transplanted from Germany to the United States. As discussed in the previous chapter, Melanchthon's code, which set the pattern for much Protestant educational thinking, envisioned a three-tiered school system. The compulsory *Volksschule* provided German children their initial elementary education, which included a heavy dose of religious instruction. Next came the *Gymnasium*, if the child qualified, where classical languages and religion were accented. After five or six years of *Gymnasium* instruction and an examination, one might enter into the third level, a German university.[9] In America, the congregational school was akin to the *Volksschule*. The *Gymnasium* was reflected in such institutions as the Perry County "college." The demand for pastors and teachers narrowed the focus of what was taught at such schools and at Missouri's seminaries. However, early synodical leadership's vision was to have Lutheran children schooled with a solid general education coupled with theological knowledge and cultural literacy.

The school functioned to strengthen the Synod's outreach to various German immigrant groups. This was especially true in urban areas. According to August Stellhorn, these non-Lutherans ("Strangers") might constitute "50 per cent of the enrollment."[10] Enrolling children from these non-Lutheran immigrant groups frequently resulted in overcrowding, obviously making instruction more than a little challenging. Focusing on the mission opportunity, however, the Synod discouraged restricting enrollments.

One problem resulting from the remarkable growth of schools during this period was a shortage of teachers. As early as 1855 the pastors and teachers of Milwaukee established a private teachers seminary to address this shortage. The Synod took it over two years later and relocated it in Ft. Wayne, making it a separate teacher-training department of the already established Ft. Wayne theological seminary. This department was moved to Addison, Illinois, in 1864 and again relocated to River Forest, Illinois, in 1913, where it became Concordia Teachers College (today Concordia University, an institution of the Concordia University System). A second Concordia Teachers College was opened at Seward, Nebraska, in 1894 (also part of the Concordia University System today). In order to graduate, students had to pass both a written and an oral examination assessing their orthodoxy. After assessing and certifying the graduates, the faculty would then assign them to their first call.[11]

---

[9] Stephen A. Schmidt, *Powerless Pedagogues: An Interpretive Essay on the History of the Lutheran Teacher in the Missouri Synod. Twenty-Ninth Yearbook of the Lutheran Education Association* (River Forest, Ill.: Lutheran Education Association, 1972), 22.

[10] August C. Stellhorn, "The Period of Organization, 1838–1847," in *Fourth Yearbook of the Lutheran Education Association* (ed. Arthur C. Repp; River Forest, Ill.: Lutheran Education Association, 1947), 11.

[11] Stellhorn, *Schools of The Lutheran Church—Missouri Synod*, 129-150.

Little was done during this period to advance assimilation of students into the broader American culture. German continued to be the language vehicle for worship and for classroom instruction. One might speculate that the impressive growth of the Synod's parochial schools during this period may have contributed to a seeming lethargy to move forward the process of Americanization.

In spite of lethargic efforts toward assimilation, The Lutheran Church—Missouri Synod recognized a need to reach out to the four million slaves who had only recently been given their freedom. The Reverend J. F. Doescher, the Synod's first missionary to African-Americans, "surveyed the critical needs of the freedmen" and "recommended that mission stations be started with the strategy of reaching the people through the establishment of day schools." The first Lutheran day school for African-Americans was subsequently established at St. Paul's Colored Chapel in Little Rock, Arkansas, on September 16, 1878, with an enrollment of 46 students. Others were opened in New Orleans and Virginia shortly thereafter.[12]

By 1897, the Missouri Synod had grown to nearly 2,000 congregations with 685,000 members; yet, while schools still prospered, school growth had faded in comparison to general synodical growth. Including some that were only part-time agencies, school numbers had increased to 1,603 with enrollment figures at 89,202 children.[13] Early synodical school success was affected by internal and external forces that tempered congregational enthusiasm for the ideal of a school in every parish. Just what these tempering forces were is the subject of the next section.

AN ERA OF CHALLENGES

The history of Missouri Synod schools is a history of ups and downs. This dynamic reflects, among other things, the changing social and political problems encountered by the Synod in the process of gradual Americanization. Following vigorous growth during its early years, the schools of The Lutheran Church—Missouri Synod steadily increased from the mid-nineteenth century until after the Civil War, and again from 1900 to World War I. Much of this success took place within the context of challenges that tested synodical fervor regarding its schools. We will explore each of these challenges briefly.

---

[12] Richard C. Dickinson, *Roses and Thorns: The Centennial Edition of Black Lutheran Mission and Ministry in The Lutheran Church—Missouri Synod* (St. Louis: Concordia Publishing House, 1977), 136-141. The intended focus and scope of this chapter does not permit a thorough examination of the Black Lutheran educational experience in the United States. For the reader possessing further interest in the subject, Dickinson's book is highly recommended. While its treatment is limited to the Lutheran synods affiliated with the Evangelical Lutheran Synodical Conference of North America and is not limited solely to education, it still makes an important contribution to understanding this segment of the Black religious experience in America.

[13] Stellhorn, *Schools of The Lutheran Church—Missouri Synod*, 275.

The Rising Tide of Immigration

Following the Civil War a rising tide of immigration brought newcomers different from the followers of Stephan who had first settled in Perry County. Unlike the dissenters who had left Germany for religious reasons, the new generation of German immigrants came from a new Germany that

> had become strong through union and great through wars of conquest; [a Germany] launching out upon a vast program of imperialism and [that] was extending its markets into all the world; in education, literature, science, and art it was excelling all nations.[14]

In a word, these Germans were more nationalistic. However, in spite of their pride, Germany

> offered little hope of economic independence. ... The opportunities of golden America beckoned irresistibly. [These new immigrants were] flamed to high pitch by the glowing advertising propaganda of steamship companies, whose thousands of agents both in America and abroad offered ridiculously cheap rates and spread misleading information as competition became more and more intense, and attracted even more by the tales and rumors of possible wealth and the prospects of unbounded liberties and opportunities.[15]

In addition, the new German immigrants were "reared in the ... *Volksschule*, which regarded confirmation the end of ... formal training [resulting in] the idea of a general education for the youth of the Church [passing] into the background of Synodical thinking."[16]

Some of these new immigrants wanted their children to learn English, and the public school appeared to provide the vehicle to be successful in America. However, there existed an equally vehement segment that viewed the role of Lutheran schools as the vehicle to perpetuate their German heritage and supported synodical schools accordingly. The resulting tension gave rise to a controversy over language with the parochial school as the flashpoint.

The Language Issue

From their inception, English had been part of the curriculum in the Synod's schools. However, "the congregations and synodical bodies did not at all favor the introduction of the English language into the [worship] services of the church."[17] To do so would invite doctrinal laxity, "a spirit ... labeled as free, American, and undesirable" that was sure to cause young people to defect to

---

[14] Beck, *Lutheran Elementary Schools in the United States*, 161.

[15] Beck, *Lutheran Elementary Schools in the United States*, 161.

[16] Arthur C. Repp, "The Period of Planting, 1847—1864," in *Fourth Yearbook of the Lutheran Education Association* (ed. Arthur C. Repp; River Forest, Ill.: Lutheran Education Association, 1947),58.

[17] Beck, *Lutheran Elementary Schools in the United States*, 69.

other denominations.[18] There was a small group of supporters of the use of the English language. After all, as early as 1857 congregations were allowed to engage in English work when it became "absolutely unavoidable."[19] These supporters argued that the real reason for defection was the inability to understand German. In addition, some also believed that productive mission outreach to non-Germans would have to be predicated on the use of the English language. Still other supporters of English pointed to the Gospel transcending the instrumentality of language.

Generally, however, to oppose German was often perceived as opposition to Lutheran schools. Synodical publications contained an inundation of arguments promoting schools. "Superior instruction and discipline were mentioned. The importance of centering all instruction in the Word of God was an important argument. Other arguments [addressed] the evils present in public school instruction."[20]

More will be revealed regarding the Synod's attitude toward public schools later in the chapter. However, at this point it will suffice to point to the language issue as a factor in hampering Missouri's integration into American society. But it was certainly not the only factor.

THEOLOGICAL ATTITUDE

Much of Missouri's isolation possessed deep theological overtones and made its schools the foot soldiers of resistance to assimilation. Students enrolled in the Synod's schools were taught, among other things, to

- view their denomination as the one true visible church of God on earth;
- view other religious bodies as doctrinally in error;
- avoid interaction with other religious groups;
- worship only with Lutherans; and
- not marry outside their denomination.[21]

While Lutheran schools were kept on the front lines of resistance, inculcating the Synod's theological viewpoint, they also played a role in shaping social as well as political attitudes.

SOCIAL AND POLITICAL ATTITUDES

Schools taught young Lutherans to dwell upon the sinful aspects of all things secular and, consequently, to maintain a distance from the world. For example,

---

[18] Everette Meier and Herbert T. Mayer, "The Process of Americanization," in *Moving Frontiers: Readings in the History of The Lutheran Church—Missouri Synod* (ed. Carl S. Meyer; St. Louis: Concordia Publishing House, 1964), 356.

[19] Meier and Mayer, "The Process of Americanization," 356.

[20] Meier and Mayer, "The Process of Americanization," 369.

[21] Meier and Mayer, "The Process of Americanization," 362-366.

the Synod opposed the purchase of life insurance because it turned the wages of sin, i.e., death, into a profiteering business venture. Missouri would not take sides in labor-management problems. Missouri Synod pastors would regularly denounce dancing as worldly lust and pleasure. To attend the theater was wrong because "it only excited the baser emotions and was," by definition, "an institution of evil."[22]

These attitudes were partially influenced by the Synod's two-kingdom theology that divides the spiritual and the temporal into dual spheres. The latter realm serves to preserve the peace and order of humankind while the church serves as the source of divine grace and guides one to salvation. The experience with the established government church of Saxony, alluded to in the previous chapter, evidently was not forgotten and certainly was reflected in the Synod's complete subscription to the principle of separation of church and state.[23] Missouri's two-kingdom theology might also explain its seemingly rather marginal involvement in the political arena even today.

Attitude Toward Public Schools

While there were concerns regarding the evils of public schools, they were never disavowed by the Synod. Missouri's theology of the dual kingdoms allowed that the temporal welfare of society permitted the state to provide public schools. While they were to support their own school system, Missouri Synod Lutherans were obligated to provide public schools with moral and financial support. In addition, the members of the Missouri Synod were urged to exercise their influence as citizens to encourage the hiring of teachers who reflected a "Christian spirit" for public school classrooms so that the use of textbooks that contradicted the Christian religion would be prevented, and "[t]hat good outward order" would be maintained.[24] There is also evidence that some synodical leaders favored Bible reading in public schools.[25]

However, Missouri viewed public schools as being entirely inadequate from a spiritual perspective. The following 1870 indictment is representative:

> The public schools ... cannot possibly meet the educational requirements of Christian parents and the Christian church in the performance of their God-given duties. Under the law, and because of the separation of church and state, a public school is not permitted to teach either the Lutheran or any other specific religion; nor may it train children and regulate their attitudes and conduct according to any such specific faith. The reading of the

---

[22] Meier and Mayer, "The Process of Americanization," 347-352.

[23] Meier and Mayer, "The Process of Americanization," 352.

[24] Stellhorn, *Schools of The Lutheran Church—Missouri Synod*, 116-118.

[25] Walter F. Wolbrecht, "The Period of Expansion, 1864-1892," in *Fourth Yearbook of the Lutheran Education Association* (ed. Arthur C. Repp; River Forest, Ill.: Lutheran Education Association, 1947), 121.

Bible, if permitted at all, is by no means the same as a thorough course of religious instruction in a Lutheran school. Prayers, if permitted, are dangerous to the particular faith of a child, since as often as not they are formulated by unorthodox persons or by unbelievers. Even the instruction in history, geography, and other subjects can be used purposely or by default to inject in the Christian child the poison of doctrinal error and unbelief—as experience, alas! has shown. Textbooks, like the public schools, dare not represent any particular faith; they often contain various errors.[26]

This attitude, coupled with the Synod's general isolationism plus a burgeoning public school system abetted by militant Americanism, provoked the most serious challenge to Synodical schools. Beginning in the late 1880s there were repeated efforts in various states to eliminate all nonpublic schools by legislative enactments. It is to this final challenge that we now turn.

LEGISLATIVE BATTLES

Motivated by a desire to Americanize immigrant groups of all religious persuasions, in 1889 Wisconsin adopted the Bennett Law and Illinois, the Edwards Law. Similar bills with the same intent were introduced in South Dakota and Minnesota. These laws threatened to limit the rights of parents to send their children to Christian or private schools. They mandated children to attend schools in the district in which they resided. Since Lutheran schools were often some distance away, some students living within another district could be prohibited from attending. An immediate response by Catholics, Lutherans, and other religious groups brought about the repeal of the Wisconsin, Illinois, South Dakota, and Minnesota laws within a short time. However, the battle was not over. Similar legislation abolishing parochial and foreign language schools continued to be proposed in about a dozen states. After 1900, some monumentally significant battles for the freedom of religious schools ensued, particularly involving legislation governing the language and the textbooks to be used in the schools.

In the anti-German backlash of World War I, synodical schools with their bilingualism and German cultural orientation came under severe attack. The battles for the religious freedom of parochial schools in Michigan, Nebraska, and Oregon proved to be the most critical in repelling this attack. Once again, the Missouri Synod joined forces with the Roman Catholic Church and other interested parties and took the first of two of these battles to the United States Supreme Court. Ultimately, the combined decisions of the court in *Pierce v. Society of Sisters* (1925) and the earlier 1923 *Meyer v. Nebraska* case upheld the right of parents and churches to maintain their own schools and to conduct them in whatever language they wished. Private interests were guaranteed the right to

---

[26] Stellhorn, *Schools of The Lutheran Church—Missouri Synod*, 117-118.

carry on educational endeavors so long as they met the necessary state requirements and objectives.

One might argue that these legislative battles over parochial schooling were a distinctive blessing. The Synod was forced to establish more wholesome public relations and to take a good, hard look at their schools in light of public school standards. As Stellhorn points out, "A General School Board, District School Boards, and a systematic supervisory system were instituted" following the attempts to abolish private and parochial schools. Also, "[i]mproved courses of study and modern textbooks were introduced."[27]

But despite the constitutional guarantee and the Synod's reassessment of its school system, there was little cause to boast about the school situation at the close of World War I. The legislative battles and the improvement of public school systems appear to have negatively influenced the number of synodical schools as well as student enrollment. Perhaps reflecting a spirit of indifference, enrollment in Lutheran elementary schools did not keep pace with overall synodical growth. Many believed the Sunday school to be a sufficient educational agency.

Legislative threats and public school growth served to accentuate Missouri's mistrust of public education. The church was caught in a fundamental "conflict between the Christian and a pagan world view."[28] In this conflict, Lutheran schools wore the white hats and public schools wore the black hats.

Although the highest court in the land vindicated Missouri's rights, the Synod stiffened its resistance to cultural integration and used Lutheran schools to hold the line in its continuing effort to nurture its own. Whether it succeeded is the subject of the next section.

The Adaptation of Synodical Schools

Although the Synod continued to be somewhat antagonistic toward the public school, signals were emerging that Lutheran schools were blending into the American social order. For example, statistics for 1921 indicated that of the 1,190 synodical schools submitting data, German religious instruction was occurring "in only 187 cases, both German and English in 416, and English only in 487 cases."[29] The Synod's establishment of the position of superintendent of schools, the calling of August C. Stellhorn to fill that office, and the formation of a synodical school board were signs of that adaptation.[30] School supervision was obvi-

---

[27] Stellhorn, *Schools of The Lutheran Church—Missouri Synod*, 307.

[28] L. G. Bickel, "The Period of Integration, 1914–1947," in *Fourth Yearbook of the Lutheran Education Association* (ed. Arthur C. Repp; River Forest, Ill.: Lutheran Education Association, 1947), 179.

[29] Stellhorn, *Schools of The Lutheran Church—Missouri Synod*, 280.

[30] Stellhorn, *Schools of The Lutheran Church—Missouri Synod*, 295-300.

ously taking on a new importance. Stephen Schmidt suggests other evidences of adaptation as he points out, "Many teachers sought additional education outside of Synod. … The contacts between the University of Chicago, Northwestern University, and Concordia Teachers College (River Forest) were particularly fruitful."[31] Finally, in the early 1920s "textbooks not published by the Synod began to be recommended in addition to those" published by the Synod.[32]

While Lutheran schools, on the whole, weathered the storm of the Great Depression, it was not until after World War II that there was a renewal of interest in parish schools, which led to a steady growth in enrollment. The rising birth rate led to this phenomenon, which necessitated the construction of new schools and the utilization of modern school equipment,

> the development of richer curriculums … , concern for more efficient teaching, for the stating of the philosophy and objectives of Christian education, for the establishment of the office of school superintendent in more Synodical districts, and for further accreditation of schools where required.[33]

By 1961 Lutheran schools had expanded in number to 1,323, with an enrollment of 150,440 students and staffed by 5,525 teachers.[34] However, this growth did not change the purpose of these schools, at least not at the onset of the 1960s. Parish schools remained the congregation's preferred vehicle of ministry to its members' children. The emphasis was still traditional Christian teaching and nurture.

But subsequent decades have seen external forces cause an ongoing reexamination of this traditional emphasis. School quality, morality, discipline, teacher strikes, desegregation orders, busing, classroom safety, the erosion of the traditional family, and court decisions regarding religion in schools are all reflected in an important set of changes in the makeup of students enrolled in Lutheran elementary schools. For example, in 1972, 26 percent were classified as non-Lutheran, and of these 5.4 percent were identified as having no church affiliation.[35] By 1982 these figures had climbed steadily to 41.5 percent non-Lutheran, 9.1 percent of whom were unchurched.[36] A decade later, the percentage of students enrolled in Lutheran elementary schools who were non-Lutheran had risen

---

[31] Schmidt, *Powerless Pedagogues*, 87.

[32] Stellhorn, *Schools of The Lutheran Church—Missouri Synod*, 333.

[33] Harry G. Coiner, "The Purposes and History of the Lutheran Elementary School," in *Lutheran Elementary Schools in Action* (ed. Victor C. Krause; St. Louis: Concordia Publishing House, 1963), 18–19.

[34] Coiner, "The Purposes and History of the Lutheran Elementary School," 19.

[35] The Lutheran Church—Missouri Synod, Department of Research and Statistics, *1972 Statistical Yearbook* (St. Louis: Concordia Publishing House, 1973), 298.

[36] The Lutheran Church—Missouri Synod, Department of Personnel and Statistics, *1982 Statistical Yearbook* (St. Louis: Concordia Publishing House, 1983), 228.

to 49.5, with 13.4 percent having no church affiliation.[37] At century's end, 44 percent of students enrolled in Lutheran elementary schools were non-Lutheran, and of these 12 percent had no church affiliation.[38] While the foregoing statistics are skewed upward by the advent of the preschool, which tends to serve a significantly sizeable non-Lutheran population over against the traditional grade school, still apparently Lutheran schools are no longer outside the cultural mainstream. However, the external forces affecting the assimilation process raise some important issues, challenges, and opportunities as Lutheran schools enter the twenty-first century, as we shall see.

Lutheran Schools and the New Millennium

In recent decades, both public and Lutheran schools have continued to feel the ever more pervasive impact of a changing society. In chapter 9 we will attempt to explore the issues, challenges, and opportunities that stem from the changes enveloping the Lutheran school. Changing families and values are certainly representative of some of the issues and challenges that impact both public and Lutheran schools.

Be that as it may, the unifying strand running through this chapter has been to provide insight into the historical purpose of Missouri Synod schools as they developed in America. Purpose, of course, refers to a reason for being. It shapes vision that, in turn, shapes the role of the Lutheran school, i.e., that which the Lutheran school does.

That Lutheran schools share similar issues and challenges with their public counterparts is a further manifestation of the reality that it is no longer outside the cultural mainstream. The relatively recent religious pluralism exhibited by Lutheran school enrollment statistics provides a glimpse of classroom enrollments that will probably be increasingly multidenominational or unchurched as the twenty-first century unfolds.

Twelve congregations seeking a more conservative affiliation and resisting assimilation into the prevailing American culture chartered The Lutheran Church—Missouri Synod. Might it be argued that Missouri's cautious posture regarding ecumenism, among other issues, is a vestige of those conservative roots and that resistance? History teaches us that the purpose of Lutheran schools was, and occasionally perhaps still is, to reinforce such conservative and resistant attitudes. Has the consistent interaction with children and parents from this new tide of "strangers," i.e., non-Lutheran and unchurched, muddied the historic role of

---

[37] The Lutheran Church—Missouri Synod, Department of Human Resources, Office of Rosters and Statistics, *1992 Statistical Yearbook* (St. Louis: Concordia Publishing House, 1993), 224.

[38] Data made available by Ross Stueber, Associate Director of the Department of School Ministry, The Lutheran Church—Missouri Synod, January 11, 1999.

the school within the Missouri Synod? Some, including this author, believe that it has at the very least raised questions about the role of the Lutheran school, i.e., what the Lutheran school does. Do not Lutheran schools today need to be mindful also of Christ's command to "make disciples of all nations"? (Matt. 28:18–20). For example, do Missouri Synod schools need to adjust a curriculum traditionally designed to inculcate sound Lutheran doctrine? If so, how is that adjustment to be accomplished while still maintaining a distinctively Christian Lutheran school? Lutheran teachers must come to grips with the purposes of synodical schools for the twenty-first century. The challenge seems clear. The ends of Lutheran education must be relevant, clear, and understood by those who serve in them and by those who are served by them as well as by those who support them.

SUMMING UP

This chapter has attempted to demonstrate that schools have been a vital part of the ministry of congregations throughout the history of The Lutheran Church—Missouri Synod. This reflects a thorough commitment to religious education as a means of bringing up each generation "in the training and instruction of the Lord" (Eph. 6:4). The Synod's Saxon forebears came to the United States because they believed their German homeland was limiting their freedom to preach and teach their Christian beliefs. Consequently, from its inception the Synod considered purity of Lutheran doctrine essential to congregational life. The parish school historically has been the primary means of insuring the orthodoxy of future generations. While assimilation for Missouri was a gradual process, American pluralism proved to be threatening as well as friendly. The chapter concludes its treatment of the historical development of synodical schooling in the United States by calling for a fresh, clear understanding of the purposes of Missouri Synod schooling for the twenty-first century. It is hoped that the material in the next two chapters treating the philosophy and aims of Lutheran education coupled with the historical grounding provided by this chapter and the previous one will provide a foundation for a dynamic and unique vision of Lutheran schools in the new millennium.

DISCUSSION TOPICS AND SUGGESTED PROJECTS

1. In order to graduate, students enrolled in the Synod's early teacher-education programs had to pass both a written and an oral examination assessing their orthodoxy. Today only synodical colloquy candidates live under this rubric. Might a case be made for returning to the practice that *all* candidates seeking entry into the teaching ministry of The Lutheran Church—Missouri Synod be required to pass such an examination? Why? Why not?

2. In what ways have Lutheran schools become more assimilated over time? In what ways do they still fall short of complete assimilation?

3. Compare and contrast the impact of "Americanization" and cultural pluralism on Lutheran schooling in the United States.

4. Identify additional political, social, and cultural events that influenced Lutheran schooling in America from 1838 to the present. Describe the events, discuss their significance, and explain how they are congruent with or deviate from other historical forces of the period in which they occurred.

5. To what degree is it possible to have Lutheran schools respond to the forces of American pluralism and still remain distinctive?

6. Organize a group research project to examine representative textbooks and materials published by Concordia Publishing House for use in Missouri Synod schools. Identify key periods such as the 1850s, 1860s, 1870s, and other decades. Try to determine how the nature of these resources has changed over time.

7. Arrange a discussion or debate on the issue: Resolved, Lutheran schools should return to their traditional purpose of insuring the orthodoxy of future generations.

8. Write a short history of a Lutheran elementary or secondary school in your home community. Emphasize how the school has been affected by economic, social, and political trends of various periods.

9. Identify some of the major persons who have contributed to shaping Lutheran schools in America. What ideas did they espouse and what was their influence?

10. Try to imagine the Lutheran school experience your grandchildren will have. Write a brief hypothetical history of your grandson's or granddaughter's education. What current trends in Lutheran education led you to describe their education as you did?

RESOURCES, INFLUENCES, AND SUGGESTED FURTHER READING

Beck, Walter H. *Lutheran Elementary Schools in the United States: A History of the Development of Parochial Schools and Synodical Educational Policies and Programs.* St. Louis: Concordia Publishing House, 1939.

Coiner, Harry G. "The Purposes and History of the Lutheran Elementary School." Pages 3–20 in *Lutheran Elementary Schools in Action.* Edited by Victor C. Krause. St. Louis: Concordia Publishing House, 1963.

Dickinson, Richard C. *Roses and Thorns: The Centennial Edition of Black Lutheran Mission and Ministry in The Lutheran Church—Missouri Synod.* St. Louis: Concordia Publishing House, 1977.

Diefenthaler, Jon. "Lutheran Schools in America" Pages 35–57 in *Religious Schooling in America.* Edited by James C. Carper and Thomas C. Hunt. Birmingham, Ala.: Religious Education Press, 1984.

Forster, Walter O. *Zion on the Mississippi.* St. Louis: Concordia Publishing House, 1953.

Kramer, William A. "Celebrate Lutheran Schools: Their Past Signals Their Future." *Lutheran Education* 113 (September-October 1977): 10–22.

_____. *Lutheran Schools—15 Crucial Years: History of the Schools of The Lutheran Church— Missouri Synod 1959–1973.* St. Louis: Board of Parish Education, The Lutheran Church—Missouri Synod, 1975.

Kraushaar, Otto F. *American Nonpublic Schools: Patterns of Diversity.* Baltimore: Johns Hopkins University Press, 1972.

_____. *Private Schools: From the Puritans to the Present.* Bloomington, Ind.: Phi Delta Kappa, 1976.

The Lutheran Church—Missouri Synod. Department of Research and Statistics. *1972 Statistical Yearbook.* St. Louis: Concordia Publishing House, 1973.

The Lutheran Church—Missouri Synod. Department of Personnel and Statistics. *1982 Statistical Yearbook.* St. Louis: Concordia Publishing House, 1983.

The Lutheran Church—Missouri Synod, Department of Human Resources, Office of Rosters and Statistics. *1992 Statistical Yearbook.* St. Louis: Concordia Publishing House, 1993.

Meyer, Carl S., ed. *Moving Frontiers: Readings in the History of The Lutheran Church— Missouri Synod.* St. Louis: Concordia Publishing House, 1964.

Repp, Arthur C., ed. *100 Years of Christian Education. Fourth Yearbook.* River Forest, Ill.: Lutheran Education Association, 1947.

Rohde, David T. *A Compilation of Capsule Histories of Lutheran High Schools.* St. Louis: The Board of Parish Education, The Lutheran Church—Missouri Synod, 1978.

Schmidt, Stephen A. *Powerless Pedagogues: An Interpretative Essay on the History of the Lutheran Teacher in the Missouri Synod. Twenty-Ninth Yearbook of the Lutheran Education Association.* River Forest, Ill.: Lutheran Education Association, 1972.

Stellhorn, August C. *Schools of The Lutheran Church—Missouri Synod.* St. Louis: Concordia Publishing House, 1963.

Stueber, Ross E., ed. "1998–99 Statistical Report Summary, Schools and Early Childhood Centers of The Lutheran Church—Missouri Synod." St. Louis: Department of School Ministry, The Lutheran Church—Missouri Synod, 1999.

3

TOWARD A PHILOSOPHY
OF LUTHERAN EDUCATION

If one applies a "systems approach" or "ISMs approach" i.e., Ideal*ism*, Real*ism*, Pragmatic*ism*, Existential*ism*, to the investigation of a Lutheran educational philosophy, one wrestles with whether or not Lutherans indeed have a philosophy of education. Such an approach refers to complete bodies of thought that present a worldview of which education is a part. To be considered a true educational philosophy, the Lutheran position would need to present a developed perspective on such areas as the ultimate nature of reality, knowledge and knowing, values, and the requirements of correct and valid thinking. To date, it appears that no thorough systematic theoretical study of Lutheran education has been published, either from a theological or a philosophical point of view. This chapter does not attempt to fill that void. However, it can be said that "truly Lutheran *educational* philosophy is biblical theology and Lutheran thinking applied to education" and that our theology does, or at least should, influence our educational program.[1] Thus, the title selected to head this chapter.

The foregoing introduction begs several definitions. What is philosophy? With what is it concerned? What is a philosophy of education? It is to these questions that we now turn.

DEFINITIONS

When we speak of *philosophy*, we use a term that may be viewed in two senses. The first of these is that of the word itself, which literally means "love of wisdom." But to love wisdom does not necessarily make one a philosopher. Today, we think of philosophy in a more limited sense, as an individual's attempt to give meaning to his or her existence through the continued search for comprehensive and consistent answers to fundamental questions. It is this second sense of the word that makes the philosopher an active person, one who seeks answers rather than one who simply sits around engaging in speculation. Today, most philosophers are actively engaged with life. They seek answers to fundamental questions. Philosophers *do* as well as *think*, and it is their thinking that guides their doing.

---

[1] Allan Hart Jahsmann, *What's Lutheran in Education?* (St. Louis: Concordia Publishing House, 1960), xi.

What they do is rooted in the search for answers to certain types of questions and the tentative answers they have formulated.

When we speak of questions in the philosophical sense, we usually refer to three broad categories technically termed *ontology*, *epistemology*, and *axiology*. Each of these categories examines clusters of related questions.

Ontology is the category that examines such questions as "What exists?" and "What is the nature of reality?" Broadly conceived, this category inquires into such far-reaching subjects as the existence of God and the meaning of being human.

The category known as *epistemology* deals with questions of knowledge: What is truth? What are the sources of knowledge? How do we know? Concerns of this sort probe into the nature and validity of human knowledge.

The question "What is valuable?" characterizes the category known as *axiology*. Ethics is the area of axiology that studies what is morally good or preferable in both character and conduct. Aesthetics treats questions related to the concept of the beautiful. Aesthetics explores what it means to create and appreciate beauty in various aesthetic contexts.

As these and other similar questions are explored and answered in such a way as to build a logical and consistent system, a philosophy is built. "Every human being has a philosophy, a basic outlook, a *Weltanschauung*, a point of view, through which" they see the "world and find its meanings and purposes and values."[2]

How might a Lutheran deal with ontological, epistemological, and axiological questions? Arthur L. Miller offers some insight. Concerning ontology, he writes:

> As to the origin of the world the Bible describes for the Lutheran the basic facts of creation (Genesis 1:1; John 1:3; Heb. 11:30).
>
> Scripture describes also the destiny of man and of the universe. In creating the universe God established a kingdom in which He would rule and be obeyed. The fall of man brought the curse of the Lord upon mankind but God has established in Christ Jesus redemption for all mankind and all who will accept this redemption through faith in Jesus He makes once more His children and promises to them His blessings in time and in eternity. A child of God is then a citizen of two kingdoms—one temporal, the other eternal.
>
> Since it is God who has created this universe, including mankind, and since it is God who has established the relationship between man and his fellowmen there are immutable and imperishable principles involved in these relationships that are a revelation of God and which cannot be shaped up experimentally.[3]

---

[2] Jahsmann, *What's Lutheran in Education?* ix.

[3] Arthur L. Miller, "Philosophic Basis of a Lutheran Philosophy of Education" in *Thirteenth Yearbook of the Lutheran Education Association* (ed. L. G. Bickel and Raymond F. Surburg; River Forest, Ill.: Lutheran Education Association, 1956), 46–47.

Miller addresses epistemology in the following manner:

Since the Christian accepts the Holy Bible as God's revelation to man and gives it a place of authority in matters of faith and spiritual life, he regards the Bible as the only absolutely reliable and infallible source of knowledge.

It is the function of Christian education to transmit this revealed knowledge of God, and Christian education involves, then, a transmissive process.

There are, to be sure, many areas of life on which the Bible has not spoken and in these the individual is free to reason and to accept [the data provided by experience] so long as in their interpretation they do not clash with the truths of Scripture.[4]

Finally, from the perspective of axiology, he states that the Lutheran

derives much of his knowledge of good or bad from Scripture. The Bible states plainly that some things are well-pleasing to God and others are dis-pleasing to Him. Where the Bible speaks, the values are clear for the Christian.

In all other areas the Christian seeks the glory of God and the welfare of mankind. Values are determined by the extent to which they achieve one or the other of these aims.[5]

How might we then define educational philosophy? What is a philosophy of education? In light of what has just been tendered about philosophy, it could be said that "it is one's philosophy, one's world view, and one's way of thinking, applied to education"[6] or that philosophy of education is concerned with developing a logical and consistent framework through which the educative process may be fruitfully viewed.

Educational philosophizing concerns itself with many of the same questions as "pure" philosophy. Even where the questions are not the same, they are often no more than variants. For example, while the philosopher may ask epistemologically, "How does a person come to know something?" the educational philosopher may go one step further and ask, "What are the specific classroom conditions under which a person is most likely to learn?"

Philosophies of education provide a more particularized frame of reference through which to view the educational process. Certainly, education can be viewed through the general philosophical system one adopts; but if one is particularly concerned with education, it is necessary and appropriate to emphasize

---

[4] Miller, "Philosophic Basis of a Lutheran Philosophy of Education," 47.

[5] Miller, "Philosophic Basis of a Lutheran Philosophy of Education," 47.

[6] Jahsmann, *What's Lutheran in Education?* ix.

certain questions and certain aspects within the broader philosophical position in order to particularize it for educational thought.

PHILOSOPHICAL CONCERNS AND THEIR RELATIONSHIP TO THE CLASSROOM

The major divisions of philosophy have a significant relationship to education and especially to the classroom. Ontology is central to the educational enterprise because education is ultimately designed according to what a society or group considers reality to be. Different perspectives on the structure of reality lead to divergent approaches to education. Consider the distinct educational orientations that emerge from the idealist view that reality is spiritual or mental and unchanging, on the one hand, and from the pragmatists' view that reality is the interaction of an individual with environment or experience; it is always changing.

Obviously, epistemological issues are critical to educational theory. Since education deals in knowledge, the epistemological assumptions held by an educator and educational system will have significant educational implications. For example, how much contrast would be apparent between the classroom of the idealist who believes that knowing is the rethinking of latent ideas and the classroom of the pragmatist who believes that knowing results from experiencing and the use of the scientific method? The idealist's classroom would give evidence of a subject-matter curriculum emphasizing the great and enduring ideas of the culture, while instruction in the pragmatist's classroom would be organized around problem solving according to the scientific method.

There is also an intimate connection between axiology and education. After all, much education revolves around the formation of preferences that extend into the spheres of morality and taste. The teacher who espouses realism and believes that values are absolute and eternal will not teach like an adherent to pragmaticism who believes that values are situational or relative.

Considerations such as these illustrate that philosophical concerns have relevance to education generally and certainly also to Lutheran education. The responses Lutheran teachers provide to the great questions of philosophy do assist in deciding what transpires in the classroom.

SOURCES OF TRUTH FOR THE LUTHERAN EDUCATOR

But just what are the sources of truth that the Lutheran educator can tap to frame a worldview or, more particularly, a philosophy of education? Again, the two questions: What is a Lutheran philosophy? What is a Lutheran educational philosophy? The answer to these questions is not that simple. Miller's response is that a Lutheran philosophy of education is the application of Lutheran doctrine and of a philosophy compatible with that doctrine to the problems of education. A Lutheran philosophy of education begins with Scripture. It accepts the truth of God's revelation and applies reason only in those areas which the Lord has left to Christian judgment and discretion. Even in this realm of the application of reason it takes into careful account the direction of Scripture and is careful not to run counter to the teachings of Scripture. It examines the [data provided by experience] and integrates [it] into its thinking. It interprets such findings, however, in the light of Scripture, and if there is a conflict, it is Scripture that has priority.[7]

Acknowledging also that there is not a simple answer to the aforementioned questions, Allan Hart Jahsmann believes that what can be said is that "*one* of the distinguishing features of a genuine Lutheran is" the acceptance of "the Bible as the primary source and basis of ... faith, hence, truly Lutheran thinking flows from, or is in harmony with, biblical theology."[8] Regarding then the second question, what thinking can be developed harmonious with Lutheran biblical theology that would move toward a truly Lutheran philosophy of education?

A Lutheran view would provide for divine revelation, experience, and reason as the essentials for constructing an adequate, workable philosophy of education. According to Paul Bretscher, the primary source is

> ... divine revelation. In problematic situations it always seeks to determine whether divine revelation has laid down a universal principle. Discovery of such a principle determines its course of action. If divine revelation does not disclose a principle, a Lutheran philosophy of education resorts to secondary sources, such as postulates of reason and [the data provided by experience].[9]

While reason and experience are secondary sources, they are not to be ignored or belittled. They are indeed gifts of God and instrumental in "discovering objective truth, i.e., the truth about objects, both material (e.g., the eyes) and [non-material] or spiritual (e.g., the mind, intelligence)."[10]

However, Bretscher continues, while the principles or truths garnered from reason and experience are not "absolute in the same sense in which divinely revealed principles are absolute" and "are rather tentatively held principles," in "maintaining the validity of these principles we oppose skepticism, which questions the truth of every principle, as well as agnosticism, which denies all truth." Lutherans "hold to the position that in our most common experiences sensations

---

[7] Miller, "Philosophic Basis of a Lutheran Philosophy of Education," 45.

[8] Jahsmann, *What's Lutheran in Education?* x.

[9] Paul M. Bretscher, "Theory of a Lutheran Philosophy of Education," Part III of "Toward a Lutheran Philosophy of Education," *Concordia Theological Monthly* XIV (February 1943): 88–89.

[10] Frederick Noll, ed., *An Instrument for Evaluating Lutheran Elementary Schools* (St. Louis: Concordia Publishing House, 1958), 13.

do not deceive us and that things are as they appear to the senses and as reason thinks of them." God "permits man by means of his reason and by means of [experience] to discover and explore many truths which He has not revealed in His Word." But there is need for caution here because "since the Fall ... man has frequently believed in the unerring judgment of reason and in the ultimacy of [experience]." Unfortunately, history "demonstrates that even in the solution of very simple problems that surround man in his daily life the profoundest researches of reason and [experience] have frequently failed." However, to the degree "that principles derived from reason or [experience] are firmly established," a philosophy of Lutheran education would incorporate them with the proviso that they not "trespass on holy ground and that further researches by reason and [experience] may call for drastic revisions of these principles."[11] In other words, the findings of reason and experience must be used in their proper place and critiqued in the light of divine revelation. If their findings conflict with Scripture, they would need to be dismissed.

One must remember that reason "is not a source of truth in the same sense that divine revelation or experience are. Rather, reason is essentially a tool, an instrument, used to draw logical conclusions from the data provided by reason and experience."[12]

Awareness of the distinctions between the sources of truth is important to maintain in constructing a Lutheran philosophy of education. Otherwise, confusion may occur. For example, the truth of God's omnipotence is not established by reliance on experience. This, of course, is not to say that experience may not factor into recognizing God revealing himself. Does not God reveal himself, however incompletely, through nature?

Regardless, from a Lutheran point of view, there are three sources of truth: divine revelation, experience, and reason. The greatest of these is divine revelation.

> For where God has spoken, the believing, Spirit-enlightened mind and heart accepts and gives God a priority over the claims of reason and experience. Thus, when rational and scientific evidence is marshalled to deny the existence of original sin, the Christian legitimately objects, letting God's revelation concerning man's innate perversity take precedence. At the same time the Christian welcomes the gifts of reason and experience, using them to broaden his understanding and mastery of himself and of the objective world—using them, in other words, to help construct a philosophy of life and education sturdy enough to give direction to ... every activity.[13]

---

[11] Bretscher, "Theory of a Lutheran Philosophy of Education," 89.

[12] Frederick Noll and Frederick Meyer, eds., *A Curriculum Guide for Lutheran Elementary Schools*, Vol. III (St. Louis: Concordia Publishing House, 1964), 1.3.

[13] Noll and Meyer, *A Curriculum Guide for Lutheran Elementary Schools*, 1.4.

EDUCATIONAL IMPLICATIONS
FOR THE LUTHERAN CLASSROOM

Having treated the functions and interrelationships of the three sources of truth, we now consider some of the truths and their educational implications. These truths form the framework for any evolving philosophy of Lutheran education. They also provide the foundation for deriving educational aims, goals, and objectives, the subject to be considered in the succeeding chapter.

The material that follows is structured this way. Divine revelation and experience as sources of truth will be treated separately. For each, several significant truths derived primarily from that source are listed. Immediately following each truth appear one or more of the educational implications to be drawn from the truth. Because this is an introductory text, the treatment is selective and does not pretend to be complete.[14]

DIVINE REVELATION

The following are among the more significant truths derived from divine revelation and their educational implications:

1. There is a God, a supreme being. He reveals himself to us only sketchily through natural means, i.e., through the physical world and our conscience. He reveals himself to us most fully through his acts as recorded and interpreted under inspiration in the Bible, especially through the atoning and reconciling work of Jesus Christ. Through the Word we come to know God through faith in Jesus Christ.

Implications: A complete education recognizes that God is. It also recognizes that God reveals himself to us through both secondary and primary means. However, to stop with the secondary means insures an incomplete picture of God, his relationship to us, and our relationship to him. Therefore, the Bible becomes the basic tool in education, one that takes its place in the curriculum both as a subject and as a directive influence for all other subjects. Only in this way can each new generation, individually and collectively, come to know the Lord, his glorious deeds, his might, "and the wonders he has done" (Ps. 78:4).

2. God the Father, Son, and Holy Spirit created the universe and all that it contains to praise, glorify, and please him. This is especially true of God's highest creation, human beings, whom God appointed to have dominion over creation and whom he blessed with the power to subdue it (Gen. 1:26–30).

---

[14] This material is abstracted from the report of the Committee on the Philosophy and Generalized Objectives of the Lutheran Elementary School, Robert V. Schnabel, chairperson, which functioned during a curriculum workshop held by the Conference of Education Executives and the Board of Parish Education of The Lutheran Church—Missouri Synod in St. Louis, Missouri, Dec. 13, 14, 1956, cited in Noll and Meyer, *A Curriculum Guide for Lutheran Elementary Schools*, 1.4–1.10.

Although, objectively speaking, all creation exists outside of God, it nevertheless is subject to his providence, preservation, and governance.

Implications: The one great purpose of Lutheran education is to make us "wise for salvation through faith in Christ Jesus" (2 Tim. 3:15). Reconciled to God by our Lord Jesus, we live in community with one another, nourished through Word and sacrament, and strengthened to praise, glorify, and please God. This occurs when we discharge fully the earthly role that God has mapped out for us—when we become the perfect stewards of him who remains active in history. Thus the scope of Lutheran education extends to all areas of life and to all stages of life. In other words, the entire curriculum demanded by society's current structure is the legitimate concern of Lutheran education.

3. God created us with soul and body and in his image, making us holy and perfect, physically, rationally, and spiritually. God also gave us a free will. We chose to sin, thereby losing our holiness and perfection and separating ourselves from God both temporally and eternally. Since the fall into sin all human beings are born spiritually blind and dead, enemies of God, and unable by themselves to return to God.

Implications: Our special creation, our original perfection, our eternal destiny, and our oneness with others through Adam combine to make each individual of great and equal worth, regardless of race, ethnicity, or social-economic status. On the other hand, our fall into sin, our loss of God's image, and our estrangement from God make imperative an education that includes the story of God's restoration of us to our original perfection and harmony with him, thereby enabling us to use our free will to make decisions in accordance with our Creator's will. Again, because human beings—collectively and individually—are by nature spiritually dead and enemies of God (Eph. 2:1–3), we recognize that students are less than what God intended them to be, having limitations that prevent them from realizing their potential. Finally, attempting to provide moral training apart from an understanding of the restored relationship human beings have with God and the power of the Gospel for righteous living can only result in a surface morality.

4. Though we chose to sin, God remains a merciful God. In Jesus Christ, God's Son and His Word made flesh, God accomplished our redemption once and for all. Christ, in our stead, lived in perfect obedience to God's law and suffered and died to pay the penalty of sin. This redemption becomes our own when we are reborn, i.e., when we are confronted by God's Law, recognize our inability to measure up to the Law, and rise above the power of the Law by accepting through faith the Gospel promises. Such a rebirth is a work of God the Holy Spirit, who uses the Word and the sacraments as means and who empowers believers to communicate their faith to the unbelieving and to one another.

Implications: The heart of a completely Lutheran education must always be the revelation that God is merciful and gracious, demonstrating his unmerited love most fully in his Christ-centered plan of salvation for us. Since accepting

God's grace is an individual matter, the Lutheran teacher must continually confront each student with the Gospel. Furthermore, the Lutheran teacher must be one who through faith has been restored to a positive relationship with the Creator. To be an effective instrument of the Spirit using the Word and sacraments to make possible an initial and a continuing rebirth demands personal commitment. Finally, the fact that there is only one road back to God indicates that Lutheran schooling needs to be evangelistic, seeking always to share the Gospel with those who have not yet experienced it.

5. The human being who has been reborn into a renewed oneness with God is and remains imperfect in this life. Nevertheless, in and with the fellowship of the redeemed we are to be constantly growing "up into him who is the Head, that is, Christ" (Eph. 4:15). This involves a growth in sanctification, in the ability and desire to do good works, i.e., to do willingly that which brings glory and pleasure to God and which serves the welfare of self and others, both within and without the church.

Implications: Lutheran education is a lifelong process, one that is not finished until the new person achieves his or her heavenly destiny. Thus proclaiming the Gospel is never enough. We must also be nurtured in the Gospel after we have made its basic message our own. Through such nurture we are enabled to grow increasingly mature, better able to live out our new life in whatever situation we may find ourselves. This makes imperative schooling that is distinctly spiritual and that—since the whole person is to be perfected—embraces all phases of our lives.

6. Through faith and fellowship the new person becomes a priest and a member of the body of Christ, the church. As such, we have both privileges and responsibilities. Among our privileges is the opportunity to be nurtured by our fellow priests. Among our responsibilities is that of nurturing others in turn. Again, as a member of the church the new person gets and gives help in fighting to maintain the truth of God's revealed Word, in worshiping the Creator, Redeemer, and Sanctifier, in witnessing by word and deed God's mercy to communities near and far, and in sharing with others the varied burdens of life. In short, the priests of God become saints ever better equipped to carry out their ministry until the whole church is able to "reach unity in the faith and in the knowledge of the Son of God and become mature, attaining to the whole measure of the fullness of Christ" (Eph. 4:12-13).

---

[15] The New Testament knows of only two educational agencies: the home and the church. At the same time Lutherans are members of society and recognize government to be a divine institution rightfully claiming their willing obedience and support. Moreover, the Lutheran recognizes that a state with a republican form of government and a democratic way of life needs an educated citizenry and therefore rightfully assumes the responsibility to teach. Such recognition results in the Lutheran's willingness to support and improve public (state) schools. On the other hand, the Lutheran home and church reserve and exercise the God-given right to maintain their own schools because only through such schools can the home and the church effectively discharge their God-given responsibility to educate.

Implications: Each person is responsible before God for his or her own faith and education. God, however, graciously recognizes that this faith involves education and must be communicated. He has therefore delegated both parents and the church to be his instruments in nurturing each new generation.[15] As will be discussed in chapter 5 of this text, to assist both home and church to carry out their joint responsibility, God has gifted the body of Christ with a public ministry, with a corps of specially prepared and called teachers. These servants, at the direction of the body, work to equip the saints for their ministry to one another and to the society in which they find themselves. More specifically, these called teachers work to help the church become a worshiping, witnessing, teaching, and dedicated community of the elect, a community seeking the Spirit's help in its effort to grow. In short, the educational effort of the body of Christ involves all members, sometimes as teachers, sometimes as learners, sometimes as both. And its effort is directed toward helping the members to realize their potential as stewards of God's gifts—to the greatest possible degree in this life, and perfectly in the life to come.

7. All human beings have an eternal destiny either in heaven or hell, either with God or separated from him forever. However, as Lutherans we look forward to the end of our earthly lives, not despairingly but hopefully—confident that in Christ we have from eternity been elected to share the joys of heaven. Moreover, we await with anticipation Christ's second coming, the resurrection of the dead, God's final judgment, and the eternal victory God will give us. A glorious feature of this victory will be the full restoration of the image of God, enabling the saved to live eternally to the pleasure and glory of God.

Implications: One of the tensions of Lutheran schooling is that it confronts one with an inescapable eternal destiny either in heaven or hell. The Lutheran teacher must maintain an eternal perspective. The Lutheran teacher must also seek to help the student view all knowledge, thought, and action, all created things, and all the joys and sorrows of life in the light of eternity. The hope of heaven motivates Lutherans, encouraging us to witness while there is time and to dedicate our lives and talents to the service of God and our fellow human beings.

EXPERIENCE

Some truths derived mainly from experience and their educational implications worthy of note include the following:

1. Even in our fallen state we can learn. Learning involves changes in knowledge, attitude, and conduct. These changes are the result of an interrelated process involving mind, heart, and will. More specifically, learning has

- a cognitive, or rational, phase, in which we use our mental process to gain knowledge (mind/knowledge);

- an affective phase, which involves emotions or feelings and which causes us to seek what seems desirable and to avoid what seems undesirable (heart/attitude); and

- a volitional phase, in which we make up our mind to do something and the mind then uses the responding mechanisms to carry out what has been willed (will/conduct).

Implications: To effectively educate children requires an understanding of learning and the learning process. When we learn something, we are to that extent a new person. This is true whether what we learn is a new knowledge, a new attitude, or a new conduct. Of course, not all learning is beneficial; much learning is harmful and opposed to our best interests and those about us. Therefore, it is important that Lutheran schooling help students discern what learning is best for them and will enable them to glorify their Creator. Furthermore, for learning to result in truly significant change in behavior, one needs to recognize that head knowledge must motivate a change of heart, which in turn leads to a change in conduct or observable action. But for this to happen requires that Lutheran teachers and their students give attention to all three phases of the learning process; none of the phases happens automatically. Thus a complete Lutheran school curriculum includes experience that leads to the acquisition of desirable new knowledge, the cultivation of desirable attitudes based on such knowledge, and the willingness to let these attitudes result in desirable conduct and skills.

2. Learning is affected by the continuous interaction of heredity and environment. Through heredity God gives us our innate equipment and abilities. Environment, which is the sum total of all outside factors that influence our growth, helps determine to what extent the heredity factors will be developed and used.

Implications: Few if any people develop their innate, God-given capacities to the fullest. This is partly due to the debilitating effect of sin on the human organism. But it is also due to the various environmental influences that surround each individual.

Such interrelationships between capacity and environment impose several obligations on Lutheran teachers. First, they must accept children as they are, recognizing that for all practical purposes the child's potential development is limited only by the kind and frequency of environmental influences. Second, Lutheran teachers must select—and help children select—those experiences that can best enable them to develop and use their capacities in keeping with the ideal of service to God, others, and self. In short, Lutheran schools need to be concerned with environmental factors, selecting and establishing those that will foster the many learning possibilities with which an individual is gifted.

3. We can and do learn at any age. There are many different agencies of education, e.g., family, school, media, etc. The number, kind, and role of each of these agencies changes constantly, for we live in a rapidly changing world. To the degree that these agencies complement one another, our learning becomes unified and efficient. And to the degree that they relate us to the past, present, and future—both temporal and eternal—we are enabled to discharge effectively the function for which we are created.

Implications: Lutheran education is a lifelong affair. Some of this educating goes on in formal, structured situations (e.g., school), some in an informal, unstructured manner (e.g., viewing television). The question facing the key agencies of Lutheran education, i.e., the home and the church, is therefore one of how best to help the learner assume personal responsibility for continued growth. Home and church also must help learners cope with the many other agencies of education so that they can interpret and use what they have to offer in the light of their commitment to Christ.

But this requires, among other things, that home and church define clearly the role that each will play in helping the learner to learn. This involves outlining areas of distinct as well as joint responsibility. It also involves understanding the role played by the other agencies of education so that what they offer can be made to contribute most effectively to the learner's development. No one agency can do everything; each has a distinct contribution to make. The challenge is to bring all into a complementary relationship where each will support and extend what the others do. And because society is changing at an ever-increasing rate, this definition of role needs to go on continually.

4. We live in relationships. Four such relationships are basic: those to God, to self, to fellow human beings, and to nature.

Our needs grow out of the fourfold relationship in which we find ourselves. Though unified beings, we have identifiable, separate needs. These require fulfillment if we are to develop fully the abilities God has given us. Some of these needs may be felt needs, i.e., we are aware of them and seek to satisfy them. Others, though equally and even more important, may not be felt at all. These needs are spiritual, physical, mental, social, emotional, and aesthetic.

Implications: We are unified organisms and therefore grow as a whole, not one part at a time. As a whole we are greater than the sum of our parts. This is true whether the parts spoken of be physical or psychological, tangible or intangible. Nevertheless, to know and understand the parts and how they relate to one another is to have an advantage. Therefore, Lutheran teachers, though always dealing with the whole child, recognize the importance of giving attention to the parts.

The essential oneness of human beings does not preclude partitioning for the sake of gaining knowledge, understanding, and direction. Yet this partitioning is always done so that the whole person may thereby be helped to grow more consistently and evenly, ever more fully becoming a person of God and wisely, in work and recreation, making their way through time into eternity.

5. We learn best under certain psychological conditions. Among these conditions are

- an awareness of individual differences;

- a state of readiness;

- a high degree of motivation;

- a clear-cut purpose;

- a high degree of interest;

- an ability to see meaning; and

- a chance for repetition.

Implications: The psychological conditions that foster learning require attention if education is to utilize resources effectively and efficiently. This applies to both the Lutheran school teacher and student.

These psychological conditions of learning play an important role in developing, administering, and supervising a curriculum for the Lutheran school classroom. They require a classroom environment structured so that students see that God in his grace is working through Word and sacrament and through the Gospel is nurturing their life in Christ.

SUMMING UP

Philosophy cannot be avoided and it does impact our thinking, speaking, and acting. Simply, philosophy attempts to organize and systematize all knowledge around questions dealing with existence (ontology), knowing (epistemology), and value (axiology).

If you do not now have a philosophy of education, you will eventually need to develop a sound one that will enable you as a called Lutheran teacher to establish objectives, activities, and outcomes for your students. You will need to be aware of and rely on both the primary source of truth, i.e., divine revelation, and the secondary sources, i.e., experience and reason, as essentials in the construction of your educational philosophy. If you do not maintain a distinction between these sources of truth, confusion is bound to occur.

Finally, there are many educational implications that derive from these sources of truth. While our treatment was not exhaustive, the primary educational implication remains enabling your students to live in Christ as free, responsible beings praising, glorifying, and pleasing God perfectly.

DISCUSSION TOPICS AND SUGGESTED PROJECTS

1. In class discussion in this course, try to determine your classmates' ontological, epistemological, and axiological views.

2. Read and review a book on the philosophy of education. Compare and contrast selected philosophies contained in the book with material contained in this chapter.

3. Invite a philosopher of education at your university to visit your class to present his or her philosophy of Lutheran education.

4. Prepare a set of questions that can be used as a guide to interview educators—deans, department chairs, professors—at your university about their educational philosophies. Then assign members of the class to conduct these interviews and report the findings.

5. Interview an experienced Lutheran teacher about his or her beliefs about teaching and learning. Write a summary report of your findings, and then try to identify perspectives from this chapter that correspond to the teacher's beliefs.

6. Analyze an article that has appeared in a recent issue of *Lutheran Education* or *Issues in Christian Education* for indicators of a Lutheran philosophical orientation.

7. Obtain curriculum guides from a Lutheran school for a variety of subjects over several grade levels. Examine and analyze the content and identify the Lutheran philosophical grounding reflected in the guides.

8. Design a learning activity for use in a Lutheran school classroom. Be prepared to explain how it relates to a Lutheran philosophy of education.

RESOURCES, INFLUENCES, AND SUGGESTED FURTHER READING

Bickel, L. G., and Raymond F. Surburg, eds. *Readings in the Lutheran Philosophy of Education. Thirteenth Yearbook*. River Forest, Ill.: Lutheran Education Association, 1956.

Bretscher, Paul M. "Theory of a Lutheran Philosophy of Education," Part III of "Toward a Lutheran Philosophy of Education." *Concordia Theological Monthly* XIV (February 1943): 81–86.

Jahsmann, Allan Hart. *What's Lutheran in Education?* St. Louis: Concordia Publishing House, 1960.

Knight, George R. *Issues and Alternatives in Educational Philosophy*. 2nd ed. Berrien Springs, Mich.: Andrews University Press, 1989.

Nohl, Frederick, ed. *An Instrument for Evaluating Lutheran Elementary Schools*. St. Louis: Concordia Publishing House, 1958.

_____, and Frederick Meyer, eds. "Toward a Lutheran Philosophy of Education" in *A Curriculum Guide for Lutheran Elementary Schools*. Vols. I, II, and III. St. Louis: Concordia Publishing House, 1964.

Schnabel, Robert V. "The Philosophy and Generalized Objectives of the Lutheran Elementary School (Summary)." St. Louis: Conference of Education Executives and the Board of Parish Education of The Lutheran Church—Missouri Synod, 1956. Photocopied.

4

THE ENDS OF
LUTHERAN EDUCATION

This chapter, as did the previous one, examines the theoretical, philosophical, and theological underpinnings of the "transcendent spiritual idea[s] that gives purpose and clarity to learning," that which "above all, gives a sense of continuity and purpose" for Lutheran education.[1] One must first know "what one wants to achieve through the process of education. It is purpose that gives direction and meaning and value. Without ends selecting and shaping the program, education is bound to be aimless."[2]

While national and state goals for public education are often formulated by prestigious commissions or task forces, the ends, as well as the more narrowly drawn objectives, of Lutheran education have been built upon philosophy, theology, and experience as per the discussion in the previous chapter. Historically, Lutheran education harbored a strong drive for ethnic survival that resulted in ends and objectives also focusing on preserving ethnic culture and the reading and writing of old-world languages, most frequently the German culture and language. Often, it was difficult to separate culture and its most important dimension, i.e., faith.

Ultimately, Lutherans recognize that God's purpose in everything that He does is his glory and this glory is fully accomplished through eternal salvation. Thus, it might be said "that the ultimate end of Lutheran education is the glory of God and the eternal salvation of men."[3]

THE PERSPECTIVE OF A BIBLICAL THEOLOGY

What are some of the principles or doctrines from Lutheran biblical theology that provide Lutheran education with what has been its basic traditional character? The answer, of course, is to be found in the Bible that Lutherans accept as

---

[1] Neil Postman, *The End of Education: Redefining the Value of School* (New York: Alfred A. Knopf, 1995), 5.

[2] Allan Hart Jahsmann, *What's Lutheran in Education?* (St. Louis: Concordia Publishing House, 1960), 1.

[3] Jahsmann, *What's Lutheran in Education?* 11.

God's message and that provides guidance regarding the ends and objectives of an education that would be considered Lutheran.[4]

The Bible reveals that "all have sinned and fall short of the glory of God" (Rom. 3:23), that God "wants all ... to be saved and to come to a knowledge of the truth" (1 Tim. 2:4), and that "salvation is found in no one else" than Jesus Christ (Acts 4:12). Committed to the transmission of the truth that Jesus Christ is Savior and Lord and the central point of all reality, Lutheran education is a unique educational enterprise.

The Lutheran school fulfills distinctive educational ends. These ends are rooted altogether in Holy Scripture and are therefore ultimately related to Lutheran theology. An understanding of the theological bases of Lutheran education is essential for formulating Lutheran school ends. When one would affirm that the real ends of Lutheran schooling are to transmit the truth that Jesus Christ is Lord and to enable students to grow to Christian maturity, capable of serving God in every life relationship in accordance with God's will and Word, in fellowship with Christ and under the sanctifying power of the Holy Spirit, one ought to understand the biblical theology that undergirds such ends.

Traditionally, Lutheran education has consisted of efforts 1) to transmit scriptural beliefs and practices to the next generation (Ps. 78:1–8; 145:4) and 2) to nurture and edify one another spiritually (Eph. 4:29; 5:19). This is done, as St. Paul affirmed, "until we all reach unity in the faith and in the knowledge of the Son of God and become mature, attaining to the whole measure of the fullness of Christ; [that] ... speaking the truth in love, we will in all things grow up into him who is the Head, that is, Christ" (Eph. 4:13–15).

Lutheran education has traditionally been based on the recognition of the responsibility of Christians to teach the Word (Matt. 28:19, 20). Being a believer involves an educative function. Each is to share with others the gifts of the Holy Spirit. Lutheran education is the ministry of Christ's members to Christ's members for Christ's sake and in his holy name (Col. 3:16, 17). The church is the educative community that makes the educational program functional within the circle of the home and the local congregation and, on a wider scale, supports cooperative educational endeavors with other congregations (Eph. 4:1–7; Phil. 2:1–16).

Believers are under a sacred obligation to direct as God directs. Traditionally, Lutherans point to God's own standards for Lutheran education. They are

1. Education is a lifelong process. Christians are continually to "grow in the grace and knowledge of our Lord and Savior Jesus Christ" (2 Peter 3:18).

---

[4] This section is substantially excerpted and adapted from Henry G. Coiner, "The Purposes and History of the Lutheran School," in *Lutheran Elementary Schools in Action* (ed. Victor C. Krause; St. Louis: Concordia Publishing House, 1963), 3–8.

2. Education requires a comprehensive program. Whatever else may be taught, that which God prescribes has priority. The great command "to teach" also includes "teaching them to obey everything I have commanded you" (Matt. 28:19, 20).

3. Education should be effective. Humankind's eternal fate is at stake. God wants human beings to make the most of their life on earth. These thoughts are emphasized in the command "impress them on your children" (Deut. 6:6, 7).

4. Education is to include nurture and admonition in the Lord (Eph. 6:4). This involves instruction and disciplinary guidance.

Education from a conventional Lutheran perspective requires a person to communicate and apply God's Word. God calls human beings to transmit his Word, i.e., they are to provide frequent and favorable opportunities for the student to feed on the Word, to hear the Word as it is spoken, to learn the Word as it is taught, and to act according to the Word under training and discipline. This transmission of the Word is not to be a mere transfer of facts. Properly understood, Lutheran teaching is an endeavor that attempts to nourish, strengthen, protect, guide, and perfect the student. Teaching of the Word is to be related to life; opportunity is to be given to make the Word functional in attitudes and conduct (Eph. 4:11–16).

The Lutheran ethic regarding education also involves the work of God. The Holy Spirit makes the taught Word effective in our hearts (John 3:6). This must be the case because we are by nature totally ignorant of the things of God and incapable of any God-pleasing response (1 Cor. 2:14). Our faith and life are gifts. They come from outside the person, i.e., from God. The Word of God is effective, e.g., it possesses the power to lead a person from death to life. The very Word of God that is transmitted works faith in the learner (Eph. 1:19; John 17:20; Rom. 1:16; 10:17).

Traditionally, Lutheran education differs from all other education in that God himself is the creative Agent. Though regeneration and faith grow out of the educative process, they cannot be guaranteed by it. The effectiveness of Lutheran teaching ultimately depends on the power of the Holy Spirit operating through the Word (1 Peter 1:23). Therefore, the task of the Lutheran teacher is to confront the student with the biblical truth of the Law and the Gospel. This requires both an understanding of the proper use of each and the skill of rightful application (2 Tim. 2:15). The truth of human sin and God's grace in Christ prepare the students to trust God, through Christ, that they may receive the power from the Holy Spirit to live in commitment to God as his "workmanship" (Eph. 2:8–10). "Created in Christ Jesus unto good works," the "workmanship" is sustained in faith through Word and sacrament (Acts 2:42).

God is the Initiator and the Creator on whom all spiritual life and growth depend. The "new life in Christ" comes as the unmerited gift of God's grace as it is received through faith. This grace-faith relationship, rooted in biblical theology, motivates and controls the Lutheran perspective toward education. Believers are what they are because of the work of God in Christ.

God's gracious purpose is to make us "wise for salvation through faith in Christ Jesus" and to sanctify us in the faith unto every good work (2 Tim. 3:15–17). The highest ideal and end of education for the Lutheran traditionally are to fulfill this gracious purpose of God. Persons justified by grace are nurtured and trained in the Word so that they might come to full-grown maturity in Christ according to God's purposes (Col. 1:9–14). All of life is to find its center in Christ (Eph. 1:10–12). The ultimate end for the believer is life with God in heaven (Phil. 3:20).

Christ's church seeks to bring him to people so that they may come to Him and be in Him. God's purpose to save humankind is fulfilled when people of all ages are brought into a saved and living relationship and fellowship with Jesus Christ (John 3:1–17).

God's church on earth is the fellowship of the redeemed that brings Christian nurture to bear on those who have come to life with the life and Spirit of God. Regenerated persons are brought to know the fruits of repentance and faith. They are to enter into the life of the community of believers with its preaching, its sacraments, its worship, its care for all of God's creation, its concern for missionary work and teaching the faith, and its care for the churches. Regenerated persons are to worship, work, pray, and give for the welfare and spread of Christ's kingdom. They know that this is God's world, that they have a stake in it, that God made them and called them for himself and redeemed them in Christ to be his own and called them to serve him (Titus 2:14). Regenerated individuals are enabled to trust the Holy Spirit's creative power and so receive the gift of faith and the ability to obey God and to grow in knowledge and grace and love (2 Cor. 9:8; Rom. 6:4–11). They can be certain of their justification before God at all times and look hopefully to being with God in heaven forever (2 Tim. 1:12).

God's revealed, communicated, received, and believed Word answers an individual's fundamental questions about human existence. Lutherans believe that the human dilemma today is due to our inability to make up our minds as to who we are and what we should do with our lives (1 Cor. 2:9). We are not as God, intended us to be, i.e., in his likeness. We are, rather, completely unlike God with our original divine image ruined beyond our ability to amend it (Eph. 2:3).

Lutheran theology affirms that the human creature, made in the divine image, is a person who was and is a sinner (Gal. 5:17). The human creature is in a dreadful predicament apart from God. Therefore, the traditional emphasis in Lutheran education is not on our goodness or our ability to save ourselves. Rather the emphasis is on God, who in great love planned a means by which we may be salvaged and have his life reestablished within us. Jesus, God's Son, was sent into the world to redeem us, to suffer and die on the cross so that God could forgive our sins and send his Spirit back into our hearts (John 3:1–16).

Redeemed, regenerated sinners are faced with the problem of combat for the rest of their lives. The flesh, born of flesh, constantly pulls down and away from God. The spirit, born of the Holy Spirit, strives upward and toward God. Children of God must be armed with the Word, which is the power of God unto salvation. This is the only power that can enable us to overcome the conditions of human experience and existence that bind us, because of our very nature, earthward. This is the only power that can make the rule of God functional in our lives, hearts, wills, and minds, enabling us to become what God wills us to be (Eph. 6:10, 11; Gal. 2:20).

Lutherans use the educative process to unfold to humankind the truth of God. We cannot find an adequate solution to the deepest needs and questions within us. We need to know who we are and how we are in our finiteness and sin. We need to know who other people are and how we are to be related to them. We need to know what the purpose of life is, where we are going in eternity, and what we are and may become by reason of Jesus Christ. The answers to our questions and problems, as we struggle for truth, life, and good, depend wholly on those redemptive events through which God gives us power to do that which we cannot accomplish of ourselves. God's gracious Word breaks through our defenses and prepares our hearts to receive answers to the deepest and most persistent questions arising in human existence (Eph. 2:19–22).

The ends of Lutheran education, as already indicated, are derived from Holy Scripture. Lutheran education transmits God's Word, fulfills God's purpose for us, and addresses the problems of human existence. Therefore, Lutheran schools are maintained, in part, to fulfill the God-ordained ends of Christian teaching and nurture.

The program of the Lutheran school, consequently, is determined and implemented in relation to the ends of Lutheran education. The specific objectives are rooted in biblical theology.

A theological orientation is helpful when discussing the role of the Lutheran school in fulfilling the ends of Lutheran education. For example, Lutheran schooling is based on a scriptural view of God, the human being, the world, life, faith, reason, character, personality, experience, and death. Viewing such vital concerns scripturally leads to certain conclusions. Truly Lutheran schooling requires an understanding of the ultimate aim of human life and a clear idea of what we are and what God intends us to become. Armed with this understanding, Lutheran schools can properly and effectively create a Bible-based, Christ-centered, and life-directed learning environment.

Ultimately, it's the Gospel that forms the base for Lutheran schools. The good news that God loves and forgives gives meaning for the very existence of all levels of formal Lutheran schooling—early childhood, elementary, junior high or middle school, secondary, and higher education.

THE OBJECTIVES OF LUTHERAN EDUCATION

From the traditional Lutheran perspective,

> The ultimate aim of Lutheran education is co-extensive with the ultimate purpose of life. Education, in all its aspects, should be not simply "neutral" with respect to the ultimate purpose of life. Rather, education should make a positive, constructive contribution toward the fulfillment of this ultimate purpose. [Therefore] the ultimate aim of education ... is the praise, glory, and pleasure of God.[5]

However, conventional Lutheran reflections on fulfilling objectives have also mirrored a focus on those classified as mediate and intermediate goals. Frederick Nohl described the mediate objective of Lutheran schools in these words.

> Sin blocks the attainment of the ultimate objective. Fallen man, having lost God's image and perfect fellowship with God, cannot praise, glorify, and please his Creator. Natural man must first regain God's image and resume the fellowship that once existed. Therefore the mediate objective of [Lutheran] education is: That the child may regain God's image and an unending fellowship with God.[6]

Proceeding from the general to the more specific, the following two intermediate objectives, "both indispensable to attaining the mediate and ultimate objectives," were set forth by Nohl: "a. That the child knows and trusts in the true God, knows what God requires of him, and knows and trusts in what God has done for him in Christ," and "b. That the regenerated child grows in grace, i.e., in a life of good works."[7] In addressing how a person might arrive at these intermediate objectives, Nohl stated:

> Sin also blocks the attainment of the mediate objective. By himself man is unable to regain God's image and resume fellowship with God. God Himself must take the initiative. God has done this by sending His Son to save all men. God proclaims this redeeming act in His Word, sending His Spirit to create faith in the hearts of individuals. Finally, God continues to operate through His Word and Sacraments, carefully nurturing the regenerated

---

[5] Robert V. Schnabel, "The Philosophy and Generalized Objectives of the Lutheran Elementary School (Summary)" (St. Louis: Conference of Education Executives and the Board of Parish Education, The Lutheran Church—Missouri Synod, 1956), photocopied, 15.

[6] Frederick Nohl, ed., *An Instrument for Evaluating Lutheran Elementary Schools* (St. Louis: Concordia Publishing House, 1958), 25.

[7] Nohl, *An Instrument for Evaluating Lutheran Elementary Schools*, 26.

Christian's growth in grace. In all of this, however, the home and the church, acting as God's agents, play a vital role.[8]

It is these considerations that lead to the two aforementioned intermediate objectives.

We turn now to the most specific category of traditional objectives for Lutheran schooling, those that the education programs are to be aimed at most directly, i.e., determining learning activities and desired outcomes, and providing a foundation for assessing Lutheran school effectiveness. In doing so, we find that there exist Lutheran statements of immediate goals constituting four types arranged according to the basic relationships in which one finds oneself as a believer. We must first of all live with God, then with ourselves and our own God-given powers, and finally with others and with God's creation (nature).[9]

These immediate objectives, as set forth by Nohl, are as follows:

1. In terms of their relationship to God, the Lutheran school attempts to help the student develop

   - a growing knowledge of the Triune God, a growing trust in Jesus Christ as the Savior from sin, and an increasingly sanctified life.

   - a growing knowledge of the Holy Scriptures as the Word of Life, a proper understanding of Law and Gospel and an increased ability to apply God's Word to life situations, and a desire to gain the blessings of Holy Baptism and the Lord's Supper.

   - an understanding of the nature, function, and responsibility of the church as the body of Christ, plus a willingness and ability to serve as an active member of that body and as a priest of God.

2. Concerning the student's relationship to self, the Lutheran school seeks to help those enrolled

   - develop knowledges, attitudes, and conducts needed to function effectively as God's children (spiritual powers).

   - understand their body and accept responsibility for its health, safety, and recreation (physical powers).

   - develop logical, scientific, and creative thinking habits, gain knowledge and communication tools, and acquire significant elements of their cultural heritage (mental powers).

   - develop social skills required to function competently and creatively (social powers).

---

[8] Nohl, *An Instrument for Evaluating Lutheran Elementary Schools*, 25–26.

[9] Nohl, *An Instrument for Evaluating Lutheran Elementary Schools*, 26.

- understand and control their emotions, find security and a true picture of themselves through firm reliance on God and trust in Christ, and practice Christian love toward all human beings (emotional powers).

3. In addressing the student's relationship toward others, the Lutheran school attempts to assist its charges that they may

   - recognize all people to be God's creation and show respect, courtesy, and consideration for the rights and welfare of others.

   - respect parents as God's representatives and appreciate their privileges and responsibilities as a member of a family of which God is the Head.

   - develop Christian social responsibility and cooperative skills.

   - develop concern for the spiritual and material welfare of all people and show this concern through witnessing and welfare activities.

   vrespect government as ordained by God and appreciate their privileges and responsibilities as a member of the community, state, nation, and world.

4. Students' relationship to nature will be so fostered by the Lutheran school that they will

   - understand that God is the Creator, Ruler, and Preserver of nature.

   - thank and praise God for the gifts of nature.

   - develop knowledges, attitudes, and conducts needed to understand, use, and care for God's gifts in nature.

   - willingly use nature to glorify God and serve others.[10]

Meyer and Rast subsequently also included the above relationships in their organization scheme of immediate objectives for Lutheran schooling, but the believer's relationship or life with God is set apart from their relationship toward the Bible and toward the church. While admittedly it might "be difficult to establish a relationship with … a book," the need to "define a relationship with the Bible" is paramount "because the Bible is one means by which" a student enrolled in a Lutheran school "comes to know God." According to Meyer and Rast, the importance of organizing the Lutheran school's immediate objectives around the church becomes apparent when it is understood that

> The church includes the whole family of God in all times and all places. It cuts across all human divisions and organizations such as family, community, race, and nation. The child's first concept of church is most likely in the family. As [the child] matures [the child] includes in this circle his [or her] school … friends, his [or her] congregation and denomination, and finally God's people throughout the world. The Body of Christ concept found in

---

[10] Nohl, *An Instrument for Evaluating Lutheran Elementary Schools*, 25–26.

Scripture best describes the relationships to be developed in the church. In a body each member has its function to perform in support of the others. So it is in the church. Each member functions to support, comfort, forgive, and reconcile the others in full confidence and selflessness, knowing that both the status and future of each member is assured. Freedom, love, acceptance, and forgiveness are key marks of this relationship.[11]

While much of the literature treating the ends and objectives of Lutheran schooling has had a generic focus or a focus colored by the elementary level, there have been attempts to set forth objectives for the high school as well. The following litany of objectives reflects the perspective of Paul Lange, a leading figure in the evolution of Lutheran secondary education, regarding the subject.

1. The dynamic central purpose of a Lutheran high school is to impart to the students a growing knowledge of the grace of God in Christ Jesus, their Savior, and his consequent gracious will tending to their sanctification (Heb. 5:13-14; Eph. 3:16-19; 2 Peter 3:17-18).

2. To encourage, on the basis of Scriptural knowledge, a complete and harmonious development of the student's capabilities of body and soul for the service of God and [humankind] in home, church, and state.

   a. To create strength for sanctified living by encouraging
      * daily searching the Scripture;
      * daily and fervent prayer;
      * regularly partaking of the Lord's Supper;
      * regularly attending church services.

   b. To develop sincere, consecrated Christians by
      * submitting to the governance of God;
      * facing with Christian strength all trials and tribulations;
      * practicing Christian virtues, such as honesty, faithfulness, humility, etc.;
      * accepting humbly and with thanksgiving material blessings from God.

   c. To acquire a good acquaintance with the distinctive doctrines, history, and organization of the Lutheran Church by
      * acquiring the ability to defend Bible doctrines against false teachings;
      * developing an independence in Bible interpretation through searching and critical thinking;
      * showing a deepened Lutheran consciousness;
      * developing a sense of "belonging" and "at-home-ness" in the work of the church.

---

[11] Frederick A. Meyer and Harold W. Rast, *Foundations for Christian Education* (St. Louis: Board of Parish Education, The Lutheran Church—Missouri Synod, 1971), 30.

  d. To develop a zeal for the promotion of God's kingdom by
   - working as a member of the local congregation;
   - willingly giving for the promotion of God's kingdom;
   - developing an interest in mission work.

  e. To promote personal and social adjustment on the basis of Scripture by
   - an intelligent adjustment to a changing physical body;
   - a new orientation to age mates, learning to deal with people as one's equals;
   - gaining a new orientation to the opposite sex;
   - establishing a degree of independence from one's parents and becoming a part of a new family (the goal is affection for parents without dependence upon home);
   - achieving a satisfactory economic and social status;
   - developing a functional code of Christian ethics.

  f. To develop a genuine love for family life in a Christian home and an understanding of parenthood by
   - respecting parents and superiors as God's representatives;
   - treating family members with love and Christian consideration;
   - accepting responsibilities as a member of a Christian home;
   - preparing for duties of parenthood.

  g. To train God-fearing citizens so that they may take their place as effective members of the community and the state by
   - accepting government as God-ordained;
   - recognizing their duty toward community and the state;
   - developing a willingness to participate in civic affairs;
   - recognizing public office as a sacred trust and responsibility to God.

3. To transmit in a measure the cultural heritage of the past so that the accomplishments of former generations might be appreciated and an understanding of the problems of the present might be gained.

4. To develop a satisfactory competence in the literacy skills and a continuing interest in the cultural aspects of living.

5. To foster the development of good work habits and the skills necessary for critical thinking.

6. To prepare students for vocational activities necessary for earning a livelihood.

7. To foster physical health and desirable health habits.

8. To encourage the acquisition of social amenities necessary to wholesome human relations.

9. To encourage a worthy and God-pleasing use of leisure time.

10. To develop an adequate understanding of and a deep interest in Lutheran Christian education at all levels as a vital function of the home and the church.[12]

In addition to being influenced by the perspective of biblical Lutheran theology, the Lutheran school, as a social institution along with its objectives, has been and continues to be influenced by external social forces. While traditionally the objectives of Lutheran schooling paid lip-service to the function of mission, societal change initiated further thinking regarding the prominence of Lutheran schools in evangelism. For most of its history, the Lutheran school's principal function was to train *Lutheran* children in the way of the Lord, keep the German ethnic heritage strong, and perpetuate the common German language. However, as indicated in chapter 2, relatively recent and often volatile issues impacting American education, such as school quality, morality, discipline, teacher strikes, desegregation orders, busing, classroom safety, the erosion of the traditional family, and court decisions regarding religion in schools, have changed our understanding concerning the objectives and ends of Lutheran schooling. Parents, who seek options in order to avoid the above societal realities and whose motives are often secular and materialistic, are flocking to Lutheran schools to seek a private education. These non-Lutheran and non-Christian students are being viewed as potential members of the Lutheran family, i.e., mission prospects, and have caused an ongoing reexamination of Lutheran schooling's ends and objectives.

A biblical theology of mission has evolved that still acknowledges the Lutheran school's primary end of promoting and nurturing the faith, but that also stresses the Great Commission: "Therefore go and make disciples of all nations, baptizing them in the name of the Father and of the Son and of the Holy Spirit, and teaching them to obey everything I have commanded you. And surely I am with you always, to the very end of the age" (Matt. 28:19–20). The main command or goal of the Great Commission is "to make disciples" and is accomplished by "going," "baptizing," and "teaching."

Understanding "God's Education Manifesto as ... 'making disciples'" changed the Lutheran school paradigm. No longer is the end of Lutheran

---

[12] Paul W. Lange, "The Objectives of Lutheran Secondary Education," in *Thirteenth Yearbook of the Lutheran Education Association* (ed. L. G. Bickel and Raymond F. Surburg; River Forest, Ill.: Lutheran Education Association, 1956), 129–130. It is interesting to compare this list of objectives for Lutheran secondary education, published in 1957, with the seven goals of secondary education compiled by the National Education Association's Committee on the Reorganization of Secondary Education in 1918. While the listing reflects a biblical Lutheran theological perspective, it also reflects the seven *Cardinal Principles of Secondary Education* that included not only intellectual development, but also education in health, family living, vocation, civics, use of leisure time, and ethics. Also interesting to note are some remaining vestiges of progressive education's last gasp, i.e., the movement called "Life Adjustment Education," that were soon to receive a barrage from such conservative critics as Arthur Bestor, Hyman Rickover, and Max Rafferty, facilitated, in part, by the launching of Sputnik in 1957.

schooling to "just teach, or only share the faith"; now a purpose of the school is to focus upon non-Lutheran and non-Christian parents and students "becoming responsible members of the body of Christ—disciples" through the work of the Holy Spirit. "The Great Commission is not fulfilled" simply by perfunctory acts of teaching and baptizing. One mission theology holds that the end of Lutheran schooling is not accomplished "until the person becomes a responsible member of the body of Christ."[13]

In traditional Lutheran thinking, nurture is an end. Viewing Lutheran schooling from the perspective of a theology of mission results in nurture becoming "a means to an end" in reaching "out to the non-Lutheran student." In applying a mission theology, the end of the Lutheran school remains that of providing Lutheran Christian education, "to apply religion to all its subjects and human relationships. In addition," there exists the end "of outreach to the entire family, to win them for Christ and invite them into the community of Christ." The Lutheran school's end is to fulfill "the Great Commission: to make disciples of all people." It teaches students *about* church but" also teaches "them to *be* the church."[14]

For the Lutheran school, "making disciples" means 1) "teaching" students "about the Christian life, and teaching them how to experience the Christian life around the Word and sacraments"; 2) "teaching" students "what the Bible says, and also teaching them how to study and read the Bible"; 3) "teaching" students "that God wants their time, talents, and treasures, and also helping them to discover their gifts and use them for service to God"; and 4) "teaching them the Gospel, but also equipping and training them to share the Gospel." Permeating the love of Jesus Christ, the end of Lutheran schooling "is to equip people for ministry so that they might become the church in the world."[15]

WHY LUTHERAN SCHOOLS?

So then, given the cost, why Lutheran schools?[16] While the emphasis on mission has risen in prominence, traditional ends for Lutheran schools, excepting the preservation of the German culture and language, appear to remain somewhat constant. After all, the need to teach the life-giving and sustaining Word of God is as pressing as ever.

---

[13] Kent R. Hunter, *The Lutheran School: Opportunity for Mission* (St. Louis: Board for Evangelism and Board of Parish Education, The Lutheran Church—Missouri Synod, 1979), 3–6.

[14] Hunter, *The Lutheran School*, 7.

[15] Hunter, *The Lutheran School*, 7.

[16] This is excerpted and adapted from Ross E. Stueber, *Lutheran School Administrator's Handbook: Why the Lutheran School* (St. Louis: School Service Department, The Lutheran Church—Missouri Synod, 1995), 4–7.

The following are among the primary contemporary ends of Lutheran schooling as set forth by current synodical leadership:

1. *To Nurture Faith.* For those who have heard the Gospel news of Jesus Christ and believe already, there is a continued need to study it for growth and nurture. While the Holy Spirit performs his gracious work through the Gospel, there is also a need to turn back to God on a daily basis. The only means—the power—for bringing repentance comes from the Gospel of reconciliation and forgiveness in Christ (Rom. 1:16).

2. *To Grow in Grace and Knowledge.* Peter urged believers to "grow in the grace and knowledge of" the "Lord and Savior Jesus Christ" (2 Peter 3:18). This exhortation recalls Jesus' prayer the night before his crucifixion: "Now this is eternal life: that they may know you, the only true God, and Jesus Christ, whom you have sent" (John 17:3). The Lutheran school provides opportunities *all day long* to come to know him who is the "way, the truth, and the life" in a close and personal way. It is the Lutheran teacher who makes sure this occurs and sets the tone for what happens in the Lutheran school classroom. Lutheran teachers are convinced that the Bible is God's Word, know Jesus Christ as their personal Savior, and are committed to sharing that news each day with their students. The Gospel permeates the entire curriculum, not just the religion class. Of course, it is only through the Holy Spirit, working through the Word and sacraments, that the will is changed to conform more closely to the will of Christ.

3. *To Saturate with the Word.* God's people are directed to instruct children in the Word on an around-the-clock basis. They are to teach the words God has commanded. They are to "impress them on [the] children. Talk about them when [they] sit at home and when [they] walk along the road, when [they] lie down and when [they] get up" (Deut. 6:7). This charge was given not just to parents. All Israel received it. Clearly, the leaders were to make every effort to let the Word of God permeate and saturate the entire life of God's people. Given the realities of modern parenting, the Lutheran school is an extremely important cog in providing instruction in the Word on a continual basis.

4. *To Communicate and Establish Christian Values.* The Lutheran school provides an environment where the Word of Truth can produce a reverence and love for God, knowledge of salvation, passion for justice, desire for peace, and concern for the poor and oppressed of this world.

5. *To Equip for Christian Service.* Lutheran schools help students to see how their life's work—whatever it may be—can be used in the Lord's service. As members of the body of Christ, each has a task to perform in building the body. Equipping saints for Christian service is a prime task of the Christian church,

fulfilled at least in part through the Lutheran school. In fact, the Lutheran school is the church in action, not something separate from it. The Lutheran school is the body of Christ in that particular location, carrying out its work of mutual service and upbuilding. As Christ said, "For where two or three come together in my name, there am I with them" (Matt. 18:20). There the Word is being shared. There Christ's work is being carried on.

6. *To Reach Out.* Mission refers to sharing the Gospel with those who have never heard it before, or who have heard it but have not come to faith. Lutheran schools exist to share the love of Christ, expressing their commitment to reach out to others. Lutheran schooling is an effective means to this end. Both students and their families have been brought to Jesus Christ through the Lutheran school. Every year students are baptized as a direct result of Lutheran schools at various levels—early childhood, elementary, junior high or middle school, and high school—reaching out.

One senses in the foregoing an amalgam of traditional and more expansive ends for contemporary Lutheran schooling. Be that as it may, Lutherans continue to believe that formal full-time preschools, elementary and secondary schools, and universities remain the most effective agencies for equipping for ministry that are available to the church body.

Summing Up

The ends as well as the objectives of Lutheran education derive from God's Word as contained in the Bible. Traditionally, part of the reason Lutheran schools existed was to accomplish God's command to nurture and teach the faith. More recently, a biblical theology of mission has expanded this conventionally narrower view of the ends and objectives of Lutheran schools.

Lutheran schools remain a vital cog in both the formal and the informal education of the students put into their care. Today, the ends of Lutheran schools focus on education, worship, evangelism, fellowship, and service.

Discussion Topics and Suggested Projects

1. Visit a Lutheran school and ask to examine its mission statement. What plans do the teachers and administrators have to achieve their goals?

2. Many Lutheran school faculty members now work collaboratively to develop school mission statements or to do schoolwide strategic planning. Invite representatives from a Lutheran school that has gone through such a process to talk to the class about their experiences and about the goals for their school that they have identified. How and why did they choose the goals they did, and what are they doing to implement their goals? Have they encoun-

tered any barriers to achieving their goals? If so, what are they and what do they need to overcome them?

3. Examine goals and objectives in several curriculum guides from a Lutheran school. Do you think they would provide guidance to the school administrator and teachers at the school?

4. Interview a practicing Lutheran teacher. How important or useful does he or she think the following are to effective Lutheran classroom teaching: 1) principles or doctrines from Lutheran biblical theology, 2) schoolwide objectives, and 3) general and specific instructional objectives for teaching. Write a report of your findings. Conclude your report with your own opinions on the questions. Do you agree or disagree with the teacher? Why? Compare and contrast your report with those of your classmates.

5. Write Goals 2020 for Lutheran schools. Be as idealistic as you like, but also realistic.

6. In your opinion, do Lutheran educational ends tend to stress the private (e.g., personal salvation) to the detriment of also facilitating the creation of a public mind?

RESOURCES, INFLUENCES, AND SUGGESTED FURTHER READING

Bickel, L. G., and Raymond F. Surburg, eds. *Readings in the Lutheran Philosophy of Education. Thirteenth Yearbook.* River Forest, Ill.: Lutheran Education Association, 1956.

Coiner, Harry G. "The Purposes and History of the Lutheran Elementary School." Pages 3–20 in *Lutheran Elementary Schools in Action.* Edited by Victor C. Krause. St. Louis: Concordia Publishing House, 1963.

Hunter, Kent R. *The Lutheran School: Opportunity for Mission.* St. Louis: Board for Evangelism and Board of Parish Education, The Lutheran Church—Missouri Synod, 1979.

Jahsmann, Allan Hart. *What's Lutheran in Education?* St. Louis: Concordia Publishing House, 1960.

Meyer, Frederick, and Harold W. Rast. *Foundations for Christian Education.* St. Louis: Board of Parish Education, The Lutheran Church—Missouri Synod, 1971.

Nohl, Frederick, ed. *An Instrument for Evaluating Lutheran Elementary Schools.* St. Louis: Concordia Publishing House, 1958.

Postman, Neil. *The End of Education: Redefining the Value of School.* New York: Alfred A. Knopf, 1995.

Schnabel, Robert V. "The Philosophy and Generalized Objectives of the Lutheran Elementary School (Summary)." St. Louis: Conference of Education Executives and the Board of Parish Education of The Lutheran Church—Missouri Synod, 1956. Photocopied.

Stueber, Ross E. *Lutheran School Administrator's Handbook: Why the Lutheran School.* St. Louis: School Service Department, The Lutheran Church—Missouri Synod, 1995.

5

THE LUTHERAN TEACHER
AS MINISTER

The office of the Lutheran teacher is unique in that it is part of the public ministry of the church. It is one of a number of offices through which a congregation discharges its public ministry of the Word. These offices call for functions that not only are necessary but that only the church performs as an institution. Thus, the teaching of the faith in a Christian school is a function unique to the church. Properly speaking, a professional, trained teacher who is called as a teacher by the church may be said to be performing a function of the office of the public ministry.[1] Theologically and practically, this has been the consistent view of The Lutheran Church—Missouri Synod as it relates to the status of the Lutheran teacher as minister.

However, just as there has been a debate regarding the status of public school teachers in American society, there has also been a parallel discussion within the Missouri Synod concerning the status of the Lutheran teacher. Within the context of public education, the concern has been focused on whether teaching can be considered, in the fullest sense, a profession. Within Missouri, the issue appears to center on the hierarchy among the various offices through which a congregation performs its public ministry of the Word. As an aspect of ministry, the office of the Lutheran teacher is a profession.

Relying heavily on the primary and secondary literature on the topic, this chapter attempts to document the chronological history of various selected viewpoints regarding the issue of teacher as minister. The treatment is not meant to be exhaustive, merely representative or illustrative.[2]

---

[1] Report of the Commission on Theology and Church Relations, "The Ministry: Offices, Procedures, and Nomenclature" (St. Louis: The Lutheran Church—Missouri Synod, September 1981), 18.

[2] For a thorough examination of the role of the Lutheran educator in relation to the church's ministry, the reader is directed to Robert M. Toepper's three-part series "Is the Lutheran Teacher a Minister? Yes, But … . The Question of Teacher Ministry in Historical Perspective" in *Lutheran Education* 131 (November-December 1995, January-February 1996, and May-June 1996): 62-79, 124-142, and 249-268. This chapter is a condensed version of that more expansive study conducted by Toepper exploring some of the uncertainties and ambiguities of the teaching ministry over which the Missouri Synod has agonized.

Walther's Position and the Early Institutionalization of the Teacher as Auxiliary Minister

The Missouri Synod's position on ministry was conceptualized in "The Theses on the Ministry," a doctrinal work prepared by the Reverend Dr. C. F. W. Walther, one of the Synod's founders, and approved by the Synod in 1851. The ten theses are as follows:

Thesis I

The holy ministry, or the pastoral office, is an office from the priestly office, which belongs to all believers.

Thesis II

The ministry, or the pastoral office, is not a human ordinance, but an office established by God Himself.

Thesis III

The ministry of preaching is not an arbitrary office, but its character is such that the Church has been commanded to establish it and is ordinarily bound to it till the end of days.

Thesis IV

The ministry of preaching is not a peculiar order, set up over and against the common estate of Christians, and holier than the latter, like the priesthood of the Levites, but is an office of service.

Thesis V

The ministry of preaching has the authority to preach the Gospel and to administer the Sacraments and the authority of a spiritual tribunal.

Thesis VI

The ministry of preaching is conferred by God through the congregation, as holder of all church power, or of the keys, and by its call, as prescribed by God. The ordination of those called, with the laying on of hands, is not by divine institution but is an apostolic ordinance and merely a public, solemn confirmation of the call.

Thesis VII

The holy ministry is the authority conferred by God through the congregation, as holder of the priesthood and of all church power, to administer in public office the common rights of the spiritual priesthood in behalf of all.

THESIS VIII

The ministry is the highest office in the Church, from which, as its stem, all other offices of the Church issue.

THESIS IX

Reverence and unconditional obedience is due to the ministry of preaching when the preacher is ministering the Word of God. However, the preacher may not dominate over the Church; he has, accordingly, no right to make new laws, to arrange indifferent matters and ceremonies arbitrarily, and to impose and execute excommunication alone, without a previous verdict of the entire congregation.

THESIS X

According to divine right the function of passing judgment on doctrine belongs indeed to the ministry of preaching. However, also the laymen have this right, and for this reason they also have a seat and vote with the preachers in church courts and councils.[3]

As already indicated, over time in The Lutheran Church—Missouri Synod the status of the ministry of the Lutheran teacher has been controverted. The controversy seems to center in Thesis VIII of Walther's 1851 treatise in which he states that the pastoral ministry, in the light of biblical criteria, is the highest office of the Word and that all other ministerial positions are auxiliary to it. Specifically, Walther posits that "the pastoral ministry (*Predigtamt*) is the highest office in the church, and from it stem all other offices in the church." Walther provides the following scriptural proof:

> Since the incumbents of the public ministry have been entrusted with the keys of the kingdom of heaven, which the church possesses originally and immediately (Matt. 16:19; 18:18), in order that they may administer them officially in the name of the congregation (John 20:21-23), their office must of necessity be the highest in the church, and all other offices stem from it; for the keys embrace the whole power of the church. Therefore, in Scripture the incumbents of the ministerial office are called elders, bishops, rulers, stewards, and the like; and the incumbents of subordinate offices are called deacons, that is, servants, not only of God but also of the congregation and the bishop. Of the ministers in particular it is said that they should feed the flock of God and watch over souls as those who must give account (1 Tim. 3:1,5,7; 5:17; 1 Cor. 4:1; Tit. 1:7–9; Heb. 13:17).

> Hence at Jerusalem the holy apostles in the beginning administered not only the pastoral office but also that of deacons until the growth of the congregation made it necessary that this office should be entrusted to others in

---

[3] Wm. Dallmann, et al., eds., *Walther and the Church* (St. Louis: Concordia Publishing House, 1938), 71–85.

order to relieve the apostles (Acts 6:1–6). When the Lord instituted the apostolate, He instituted only one office in the church, which embraces all others and by which the church of God should be provided for in every respect. Hence the highest office is that of the ministry of the Word, with which all other offices are also conferred at the same time. Every other public office in the church is part of the ministry of the Word or an auxiliary office that supports the ministry, whether it be the elders who do not labor in the Word and doctrine (1 Tim. 1:15) or the rulers (Rom. 12:8) or the deacons (the office of service in the narrow sense) or whatever other offices the church may entrust to particular persons for special administration. Therefore, the offices of Christian day school teachers, almoners, sextons, precentors at public worship, and others are all to be regarded as ecclesiastical and sacred, for they take over a part of the one ministry of the Word and support the pastoral office.[4]

Samuel Nafzger, executive director of the Commission on Theology and Church Relations of The Lutheran Church—Missouri Synod, is instructive here. He categorizes Walther as an example of the "mediating school" on the doctrine of the ministry. Walther's position, according to Nafzger, is between an "episcopal school," which holds that the person who holds the ministerial office is the personal representative of Christ on earth, and the "functional school," which holds that the office of the ministry is a human arrangement that functions to preach the Gospel and administer the sacraments.[5]

While Walther appeared to be stating that pastoral ministry is the top-ranking position in the church and all other positions emanate from it, the controversy relates to an 1856 installation sermon, in which Walther, as Concordia College (Seminary) president, stated that professors of secular subject matter at a Lutheran seminary serve in a branch office of the ministry. In clarifying the status of the professor's office, Walther treated the professor not as a pastor, but as a teacher of the church. He emphasized that the office of a professor at one of the church's institutions "is the office of our God" and that his cause "is the cause of the Lord." In his address, in part, Walther said:

> For God has really established but one office, namely the office of gathering, building, governing, serving, and keeping the church on earth in His name. This office the Lord ordained and bestowed it upon His church when He gave Peter the keys of the kingdom of heaven and later said to all His disciples: "All power is given to Me in heaven and in earth. Go ye, therefore, and teach all nations, baptizing them in the name of the Father and of the

---

[4] C. F. W. Walther, *Church and Ministry* (Kirche und Amt): *Witness of the Evangelical Lutheran Church on the Question of the Church and the Ministry* (trans. J. T. Mueller; St. Louis: Concordia Publishing House, 1987), 289–290.

[5] Samuel H. Nafzger, "The CTCR's Report on 'The Ministry'," *Lutheran Education* 118 (January-February 1983), 139–142.

Son and of the Holy Ghost, teaching them to observe all things whatsoever I have commanded you. And, lo, I am with you always, even unto the end of the world."

In view of that fact, this office does not only have such a large sphere of duties and such a great variety of obligations, but also requires so many various and high talents that no man is able to carry out all its phases alone, even in a limited sphere of activity. Just as the Messiah's Mediatorship is divided into three different offices, the prophetic, the high-priestly, and the kingly, so the office of the church is divided into the greatest variety of offices, calling for the most manifold gifts of the Holy Spirit.[6]

Walther continued that "their office is a holy, divine office, a branch of the office which Christ once established and ordained when he gave [his disciples, the believers] the keys of the kingdom of heaven."[7] He stated "that by the acceptance of a teaching position at this institution of learning we do not change from a spiritual calling to a secular calling, do not leave a divine office for one created by man."[8]

It is from this context that some have argued (e.g., the functional school) that Walther understood that the ministry in general was the primary position in the church and that all ministerial positions were equal branches of that general ministry. For example, according to Stephen Schmidt, Walther's address was a powerful testimony to the teaching ministry and the place of learning in the Christian community. Walther saw no difference between the teaching of secular subjects and religious ones. He saw all learning as contributory to the life of the church and necessary to the education of future ministers. He did not elevate the parish pastorate above the office of the teacher here, nor did he view teachers of secular subjects as subordinate to teachers of theology.[9] For Stellhorn, the same principle applied to the position of the Lutheran elementary school teacher. However, it must be remembered that Walther was not dealing with the office of the Lutheran teacher at this installation. According to Stellhorn, in his statements on ministry Walther at times appeared to elevate the pastoral ministry above that of other ministries and at other times he appeared to hold that all ministerial positions were branches of a general ministerial office.[10] Be that as it may,

---

[6] C. F. W. Walther, "Does a Professor of a Church College Have a Divine Call?" (Sermon delivered at the installation of the director and assistant rector of Concordia College in St. Louis, 31 March 1856), trans. A. C. Stellhorn. Concordia Historical Institute, St. Louis, 3–4.

[7] Walther, "Does a Professor of a Church College Have a Divine Call?" 4.

[8] Walther, "Does a Professor of a Church College Have a Divine Call?" 5.

[9] Stephen A. Schmidt, *Powerless Pedagogues: An Interpretive Essay on the History of the Lutheran Teacher in the Missouri Synod. Twenty-Ninth Yearbook of the Lutheran Education Association* (River Forest, Ill.: Lutheran Education Association, 1972), 31.

[10] August C. Stellhorn, *Schools of The Lutheran Church—Missouri Synod* (St. Louis: Concordia Publishing House, 1963), 462.

it is important to point out here that neither Stellhorn nor Schmidt refers direct-ly to Walther's 1851 Thesis VIII regarding ministry.

It might also be pointed out that in his 1862 theses on "The Proper Form of an Evangelical Lutheran Congregation Independent of the State," Walther stat-ed in thesis 24 that "the congregation should ... call an orthodox, godly, and competent teacher, pledge him to adherence to the divine Word of the Old and the New Testament and the Confessions of the Lutheran Church, and place him under the supervision of the public ministry."[11] Walther also told pastors that "the minister, therefore, must never forget that the teacher is one of those who minister to the church, that he conducts his office as assistant to the pastor, and in this respect, therefore, he is coordinate."[12]

Further insight into Walther's position is shown when Walther returned a series of articles submitted to *Der Lutheraner* by J. C. Lindemann, a teacher who had become a pastor and was in receipt of a call to become the first direc-tor of the Addison Teachers Seminary. Lindemann believed that the school-master was not part of the pastorate, but acted as a substitute parent, specifi-cally the father. Walther asserted that the office of the Lutheran teacher is a branch office of the pastorate.[13]

The aforementioned notwithstanding, during the latter part of the nine-teenth century and nearly all of the first half of the twentieth century, the teach-ing position generally was referred to as an auxiliary office (Lindemann, president of Concordia, Seward; E. A. W. Krauss; Herman Speckhard; F. Berg; W. C. Kohn; L. G. Zobel; and Albert G. Merkens). However, there were exceptions to this position (C. A. T. Selle; William Sihler; George Mezger; and Clarence T. Schuknecht) who stated that male Lutheran teachers were in a ministerial posi-tion comparable to the pastoral position, but which required different skills and abilities and which served a different function. During this period, it was gener-ally recognized that the parish pastor was responsible for the entire congregation while the teacher's responsibility was more limited. That the pastor was the superintendent of the parish school was generally assumed, but there were some who questioned the validity of this assumption.[14]

THE TEACHING MINISTRY IS LEGALLY CHALLENGED

In 1949 and 1950, the Synod successfully defended the ministerial status of its male teachers before the Internal Revenue Service. Further insight into the

---

[11] Dallmann, et al., *Walther and the Church*, 100.

[12] W. C. Kohn, "Christian Day Schools of the Lutheran Church," *Lutheran School Journal* 54 (January 1919), 47.

[13] Stellhorn, *Schools of The Lutheran Church—Missouri Synod*, 211.

[14] Toepper, "Is the Lutheran Teacher a Minister?" 68–78.

Synod's position regarding the ministerial status of the teacher can be gleaned from the Synod's defense.

In a 1949 spot-check of income tax returns, the claim of Mr. Eldor N. Eggen, a teacher at St. Lorenz Lutheran School, Frankenmuth, Michigan, that he was a minister of the Gospel was denied. The Internal Revenue Service expected the teacher to pay income tax on the rental value of his dwelling.

After the first appeal by Eggen and the Synod was denied, a more rigorous defense by the Synod resulted in the following statement by the Commissioner of Internal Revenue:

> [I]t appears that teaching in a Lutheran parochial school is a function of the public ministry in the Lutheran Church and that a Lutheran teacher has the status of a minister of the gospel within the Lutheran Church. It further appears that a Lutheran teacher is subject to the same rules and regulations as a pastor with respect to call, installation, discipline, and retirement; performs the same functions as a pastor insofar as the congregation which he serves sees fit to authorize him, and enjoys, as does the pastor, membership in the Synod. It is held, therefore, that Mr. Eggen is a minister of the Gospel within the purview of Section 22(b)(6) of the Internal Revenue Code. Accordingly, the rental value of living quarters furnished Mr. Eggen is not includible in the gross income of Mr. Eggen for Federal income tax purposes.[15]

At the request of the Synod, on January 25, 1952, the Commissioner of Internal Revenue ruled that the services rendered by a called Lutheran teacher were services performed by a duly ordained, commissioned, or licensed minister of a church in the exercise of his ministry and as such were exempt from Social Security. The same ruling also covered the teacher's status for income tax with-holding purposes, the wording of the two laws being exactly the same in this respect. Therefore, compensation paid to a called Lutheran teacher was not subject to withholding. According to Stellhorn, the legal brief leading to these rulings had not claimed that teachers were pastors, but that they were still ministers whose first installation was regarded, in effect, as an ordination.[16]

IDEOLOGICAL CHALLENGES TO AUXILIARY MINISTRY STATUS OF THE LUTHERAN TEACHER

During the 1940s, 1950s, and 1960s, the argument that was voiced most publicly within some circles of the Missouri Synod was that Scriptures, the Confessions, and various church fathers defined a general ministry, the *ministerium ecclesiae*, and that all ministerial positions were equal branches of that general

---

[15] Toepper, "Is the Lutheran Teacher a Minister?" 127.
[16] Stellhorn, *Schools of The Lutheran Church—Missouri Synod*, 471.

ministry. Dr. August C. Stellhorn, the first secretary of schools of the Missouri Synod, and his colleague on the staff of the Board of Parish Education, the Reverend Dr. Arnold C. Mueller, Sunday school secretary, were the primary proponents of this view. Later, in 1972, Dr. Stephen A. Schmidt, professor of education at Concordia Teachers College, River Forest, Illinois, took the position that teachers were full-fledged ministers. It is to a review of these three challenges that we now turn.

AUGUST C. STELLHORN

August C. Stellhorn, the first secretary of schools of The Lutheran Church—Missouri Synod, who served in this position from 1921 until 1960, believed that there were three erroneous conceptions of the pastorate: 1) that only the pastorate was the holy ministry; 2) that only the pastorate was divinely instituted; and 3) that all other offices of the congregation or the church were branches of the pastorate.[17] According to Stellhorn,

> There is no such thing as "only one divinely-instituted Church position" as we have commonly claimed for the present-day pastorate. On the contrary, if the positions in the early Christian church may be said to be divinely instituted, then Scripture teaches that God instituted a number of offices or church positions, none of which can be proved to exist in its original form today.[18]

Stellhorn believed that it was "wrong to confuse the public ministry with the pastor's office in the sense that only his office is a public ministerial office."[19] Instead, he held that there were many and varied offices in the church, and all led to carrying out the church's ministry. He stated that in the early Christian church there were a "multiplicity and variety of church offices" that carried out the mission of the church.[20] The New Testament revealed "a diversity of gifts and church positions."[21] Christ, in order "to perpetuate and extend His ministry in the immediate future, after His ascension, ... prepared and sent out His apostles, and also gave the Church a great 'diversity of gifts.' " Stellhorn pointed out that while the apostolate and special gifts of the spirit had been discontinued, "the ministry or office of the Church" had not been discontinued. It made no difference whether the Lord established an office directly or through his church, "it was in every case the Lord who established the office, and the office was a divine insti-

---

[17] August C. Stellhorn, "The Lutheran Teacher in the Ministry of the Church" (address to the Western District Teachers Conference in St. Louis on 13 October 1952), Concordia Historical Institute, St. Louis, 5.

[18] August C. Stellhorn, "The Lutheran Teacher's Position in the Ministry of the Congregation" (Address to the Missouri Synod Educational Conference in Seward, Nebraska, July 1949), Concordia Historical Institute, St. Louis, 3.

[19] Stellhorn, "The Lutheran Teacher in the Ministry of the Church," 5.

[20] Stellhorn, "The Lutheran Teacher in the Ministry of the Church," 6.

[21] Stellhorn, "The Lutheran Teacher's Position in the Ministry of the Congregation," 3.

tution." Thus, Stellhorn believed that the offices of the ministry in the contemporary church were divinely established, but created by the church according to its needs.[22]

Stellhorn denied that all other offices of the congregation or the church were merely branches of the pastor's office. The pastor was not the commander-in-chief with all others around him being delegated various ministerial functions to perform in an auxiliary manner. The problem with this viewpoint, according to Stellhorn, was that ministry was equated with the pastorate rather than with the mission of the church. From Stellhorn's perspective, it was incorrect to view a Lutheran teacher's office, or any other church office, as a branch of the pastorate; rather, all church offices were to be considered as branches of the church ministry, which included the preaching and teaching of the Word and the administration of the Sacraments.[23]

To those who considered the parochial school teacher's office to be an auxiliary office to the holy ministry, Stellhorn pointedly commented that "the Bible knows nothing of auxiliary offices to some other office." However, while Scripture was silent on auxiliary offices, Stellhorn was willing to admit that it did recognize that there were differences in church offices. When the apostles needed relief from their many duties in Acts 6, they created the office of deacon. According to Stellhorn, while the office of deacon was created

> ...' to set the apostles free to give themselves "continually to prayer and to the ministry of the Word," Scripture does not refer to it as an auxiliary office of the apostolate, though it was a real help to them. Rather, it was a function of the public ministry first performed by the apostles, and now given over to other church servants.[24]

It was Stellhorn's view that there was a difference between ministerial offices, but the difference had nothing to do with the degree of divinity of the office or the nature of its institutions, but only in the kind of service rendered. Stellhorn also disapproved of the concept that other offices of the church were merely branches of the pastorate because of the ranking of offices that flowed from this idea. He felt that "Scripture undertakes no ranking, and never speaks of a higher or lower office."[25]

The "call" was essential to Stellhorn's thinking about the teaching ministry "because no individual Christian has the right to work in behalf or in the name

---

[22] Stellhorn, "The Lutheran Teacher in the Ministry of the Church," 6.

[23] William C. Rietschel, "An Analysis of the Educational Ideas of August C. Stellhorn, 1921–1963" (Ed.D. diss., Loyola University of Chicago, 1980), 247–248.

[24] Stellhorn, "The Lutheran Teacher in the Ministry of the Church," 7.

[25] Stellhorn, "The Lutheran Teacher's Position in the Ministry of the Congregation," 5.

of his fellow Christians without authority from them." With a valid call in hand, the Lutheran teacher was a public minister of the church.[26]

According to Stellhorn, "the teacher's office is not the pastorate of the congregation, or any duplication of it." Rather, the teacher's primary task was the "performance of the public ministry among the children, by teaching [in] a parochial school and by activity in or through other agencies of Christian training for children." In addition, a Lutheran teacher also was responsible for other ministerial functions such as being a youth worker, organist, choir director, and a host of other activities as would be defined in the teacher's call.[27]

The creation of the office of the teacher in a congregation, as Stellhorn viewed it, relieved the pastor of certain duties that had formerly been assigned to him. The ministry of the congregation was now "divided into a pastor's and a teacher's office or offices" with the teacher serving as an aid to the pastor and, conversely, the pastor serving as an aid to the teacher so "that the ministry of the congregation be carried out more fully and more adequately."[28] The scope of the pastor's responsibility extended over the entire congregation. The teacher's office also was "an office of the entire congregation, a service to the entire congregation, and therefore, the teacher shared with the pastor a degree of responsibility for the entire congregation."[29]

In regard to women in the teaching ministry, Stellhorn asserted that "her call is just as divine as that of a pastor, male teacher, professor, and any other public minister of the Church." However, a woman was "limited by Holy Scripture to certain functions in the church on account of being a woman, and she is limited also as a teacher."[30] Stellhorn did not grant the full office of the ministry to women, but restricted the woman teacher's ministerial service "to children and women as far as teaching and training are concerned."[31]

ARNOLD C. MUELLER

Perhaps the Reverend Dr. Arnold C. Mueller provided one of the most penetrating analyses of the issue of the Lutheran school teacher in ministry. In 1964, the Board of Parish Education of The Lutheran Church—Missouri Synod authorized the publication of *The Ministry of the Lutheran Teacher* by Mueller, its Sunday school materials editor. The work was extensively researched and was

---

[26] Stellhorn, "The Lutheran Teacher in the Ministry of the Church," 9.

[27] Stellhorn, "The Lutheran Teacher's Position in the Ministry of the Congregation," 9–10.

[28] Stellhorn, "The Lutheran Teacher in the Ministry of the Church," 12.

[29] Stellhorn, "The Lutheran Teacher's Position in the Ministry of the Congregation," 13.

[30] August C. Stellhorn, "The Woman Teacher's Call—An Explanation," *Board for Parish Education Bulletin* (November 1954), 5.

[31] Stellhorn, "The Lutheran Teacher's Position in the Ministry of the Congregation," 12.

based on Scripture, the church fathers, and church practices, especially those within the Missouri Synod.

Mueller defined the two conflicting viewpoints regarding the nature of ministry within the Missouri Synod:

> Two views of the ministry have been propounded among us, and they are mutually exclusive, it is an either-or. According to one view, the pastorate is the one divinely instituted office; all other positions in the ministry stem from the pastorate and are auxiliary offices to the pastorate. According to the other view, which I believe is the biblical one, God had instituted the office of the ministry, that is, He has commissioned His church to proclaim the Gospel and administer the sacraments, but He had not prescribed forms in which the church is to fulfill the commission. All forms of the ministry, including the pastorate, stem from the one divinely instituted and all-embracing office of the ministry.[32]

Mueller continued:

> The wrong concept of the ministry was so deeply ingrained in my thinking that for months I was unable to find my way through the plethora of materials to a clear understanding of the ministry as presented in this book. In view of my experience I have said repeatedly that the person who has been brought up to think of the pastorate as the one divinely instituted office will have to go through an evolution in his thinking before he will be able to see just what the Scriptures say and what they do not say about the ministry, and why men like Luther, Chemnitz, and Quenstedt were careful not to identify the one-man pastorate as the one divinely instituted form of the ministry.[33]

In his book, Mueller used the term "ministry" to signify the general, all-inclusive ministry, the *ministerium ecclesiae*. He restricted the term "office" to denote all offices or positions in this general ministry. Instead of speaking of the office of pastor, teacher, editor, or professor, he used the term "position" to connote particular forms of the ministry, such as those just named. Each of these positions entailed certain duties, which he called "functions."[34]

In his summary of the testimony of Scripture concerning the ministry, Mueller stated that the term *diakonia* was the common New Testament term for the activity of ministers of the church. *Diakonia* was used for any kind of service rendered by private individuals, by men holding public office, and by those who were especially called to perform the public ministry of the church. It was applied to all ministers of the church who taught, administered the sacraments, and per-

---

[32] Arnold C. Mueller, *The Ministry of the Lutheran Teacher: A Study to Determine the Position of the Lutheran Parish School Teacher within the Public Ministry of the Church* (St. Louis: Concordia Publishing House, 1964), 11–12.

[33] Mueller, *The Ministry of the Lutheran Teacher*, 16.

[34] Mueller, *The Ministry of the Lutheran Teacher*, 16–17.

formed other functions of the holy office. Apostles, prophets, evangelists, "shepherds," teachers, bishops, elders, and rulers, i.e., leaders, were titles given to the men who participated in the public ministry of the church. According to the evidence of the New Testament, the ministry of the church was broader than what today is called the pastorate. Local churches were served by a number of men and there is no evidence of a one-man eldership. There was only one office of the ministry and all servants of the Word participated in it.[35]

From Mueller's perspective, the word "ministry" may be used to designate all persons who render service and thereby promote God's kingdom. This is commonly called "the priesthood of all believers." However, this ministry must be distinguished from the ministry of the servants of the Word who were specially called to serve the church publicly. Such leaders are called *diakonoi*, or servants, to indicate that the Lord has called them to serve, not to exercise authority over others. According to Mueller, the hierarchical movement that followed the New Testament period was contrary to the spirit of the Gospel, for it substituted the rule of the clergy for the ministry of humble and willing service.[36]

Mueller believed there was no scriptural basis for a hierarchy, with its distinction between clergy and laity and the clergy's assumption of power to rule over the lay members of the church. In view of their baptism, all believers are spiritual priests to whom Christ has committed the Office of the Keys. All Christians have the right to call pastors and teachers, commission missionaries, and publish religious literature in order to promote the work of the kingdom. Believers have the right and duty to teach and preach the Gospel at any time and place by virtue of their general priestly call, for the ministry in the wide sense is the possession of all Christians. The office of the ministry, the public ministry, is different from the priesthood of all believers. A Christian may serve in the public ministry only when his fellow Christians have authorized him to do so. God calls men to serve in the ministry when a local church or group of churches extends a call to the individual inviting him to exercise the functions of the ministry in their behalf.[37]

While Stellhorn gave no indication that his argument was with Walther, Mueller reflected quite the opposite. In his reading of Walther, Mueller said that one is given the impression that Walther regarded ministry (*Predigtamt*) and pastorate (*Pfarramt*) as being identical. He often used the two terms interchangeably. Walther sometimes spoke of the *Predigtamt* and meant the pastorate only. At other times he would speak of the *Predigtamt* when he was referring to a ministry that encompassed more than the pastorate.[38] Mueller was certain, however, that

[35] Mueller, *The Ministry of the Lutheran Teacher*, 38.

[36] Mueller, *The Ministry of the Lutheran Teacher*, 38.

[37] Mueller, *The Ministry of the Lutheran Teacher*, 51.

[38] Mueller, *The Ministry of the Lutheran Teacher*, 57–58.

Walther recognized only one office. Thus, Walther sometimes used terminology that indicated that he conceived of the ministry in broader terms than only the pastorate.[39] According to Mueller's interpretation of Walther, the Lord instituted only one office of the ministry, but this one office has so many functions that one person could not possibly carry out all of them. All servants of the Word, whatever functions they may have assigned to them, participate in this one divinely instituted office of the ministry. Mueller claimed that Walther taught that the office of the ministry was subdivided, and he quoted Luther as saying that the congregation determines the number of branches or positions needed for the proper fulfillment of its mission.[40]

Mueller then turned to a study of Walther's Thesis VIII. This thesis, with Walther's elaboration, simple as it was, had caused a great deal of confusion within the Missouri Synod. Walther's language, especially in the elaboration, accounts at least in part for the confusion. Walther lifted the term "highest office" out of the Apology to the Augsburg Confession and out of Luther, thereby divorcing it from its original context. Reading it in Thesis VIII in isolation gives the impression of lesser functions that are part of a higher function. When Walther used the term *Predigtamt*, which is often identified with the pastorate, it appears that he meant to say that the pastorate is the highest office in the church. Since the pastorate as we know it today was not prescribed by the apostles as the one God-pleasing arrangement for the fulfillment of the charge to preach the Gospel and since the pastorate is nowhere in the New Testament called the highest office in the church, we err if we ascribe to the pastorate alone what should be termed the highest function of that all-inclusive office called the *ministerium ecclesiae*. The Confessions, borrowing the term from Luther, identify the "highest office" with those who "labor in the Word and doctrine." In fact, Luther asserted that a person who has the office of the Word delegated to him has all the other offices delegated to him also.[41]

Mueller pointed to the crux of the controversy with these words:

> Some will say, "After reading thesis VIII and Walther's elaboration, I am convinced that Walther refers to the pastorate when he used the term *Predigtamt*." Well, we have tried to interpret Walther charitably. If he identifies *Predigtamt* and pastorate, all we can say is that he is not in agreement with Scripture, nor with John Gerhard, nor with Martin Chemnitz, nor with Luther, nor with himself. If in this instance Walther, great theologian that he was, erred, then we ought to correct his error and get back to the Scriptures and to Luther and to the great theologians who are in the tradition of Luther.[42]

---

[39] Mueller, *The Ministry of the Lutheran Teacher*, 54.

[40] Mueller, *The Ministry of the Lutheran Teacher*, 76–77.

[41] Mueller, *The Ministry of the Lutheran Teacher*, 78–82.

[42] Mueller, *The Ministry of the Lutheran Teacher*, 83.

Mueller identified a flaw in Walther's argument where Walther said that "the incumbents of the public ministry" who are entrusted with the Office of the Keys must be in the highest office because the Keys embrace the entire authority of the church. According to Mueller, preaching and teaching are the highest function of the one office of the ministry, which is subdivided into branches or individual functions or positions. Pastors do not have the authority of the Keys exclusively. Other ministers are called by the church for the exercise of specific functions that are part of the Office of the Keys.[43] It was Mueller's position that Walther certainly did not intend to take a view of ministry that would be inconsistent with the sources he quoted.[44]

Mueller continued his analysis of Walther's scriptural proof for Thesis VIII: Walther stated that the Lord established only one office in the church. This one office embraces all positions in the church. These are statements from Luther who felt that the proclamation of the Word embraces all spiritual offices. For Luther the proclamation of the Gospel was primary because the Word is primary, and the Gospel is primary because the Word is primary, and the commission of the Word embraces everything. And the pastor is certainly entrusted with this responsibility. But Walther continued: The highest office is the ministry of preaching (*Predigtamt*). With this highest office all other offices are simultaneously given. All other offices are merely a part of the *Predigtamt* and are auxiliary offices. When *Predigtamt* is identified with *Pfarramt*, or pastorate, it appears that the pastorate becomes the one divinely instituted office of the ministry and those who are professors, teachers, editors, and the like, therefore, have no divine call, since these positions are man-made.[45]

Mueller posited:

> Walther's choice of the term *Predigtamt* was unfortunate (especially since he uses the word interchangeably with *Pfarramt*), because this term is used indiscriminately to indicate either the general ministry or the pastorate. If we translate it as "ministry of preaching," the meaning remains the same. The term "ministry" today suggests the pastor's office to most people. The church should have kept the original meaning of *diakonia* in mind. As we have seen, it is Paul's expression for all types of service rendered for the promotion of the Gospel. We may, therefore, speak of the teacher's position as "ministry of teaching" just as we may speak of the pastor's position as "ministry of preaching," for both are ministers in the sense in which Paul employs the word *diakonia*. When the church again conceives of its servants in terms of *diakonia*, or service voluntarily rendered for the benefit of others, there will be no hesitancy about calling those men ministers who have devoted

---

[43] Mueller, *The Ministry of the Lutheran Teacher*, 85.

[44] Mueller, *The Ministry of the Lutheran Teacher*, 87.

[45] Mueller, *The Ministry of the Lutheran Teacher*, 89–91.

themselves unselfishly to the vital and painstaking task of laying foundations and building up the spiritual life of boys and girls in the classroom.

Walther's choice of the term *Hilfsamt*, which we have rendered "auxiliary office" is likewise unfortunate, for it has led some to the erroneous conclusion that if certain positions are auxiliary to the Predigtamt, the pastorate must be the one divinely instituted ministry. We have shown that this view is inconsistent with the teaching of Scriptures and of the theologians on the general ministry. Auxiliary offices are nowhere mentioned in the New Testament, although the deacons of Acts 6 and of 1 Tim. 2 and young men like Timothy and Sylvanus were in a sense assistants to the apostles or to the elders who presided over the congregations. The term is not used in Scripture to designate any one of the various offices of the church, e.g., those listed in Eph. 4.[46]

Mueller then attempted to determine the meaning that Walther associated with the term "auxiliary office." Mueller explained that when the pastoral duties of a congregation, like teaching in the elementary school, became too great a burden for one man, the congregation, exercising its priestly rights, often extended a call to another educated and qualified person to assist its pastor. If the second minister was a pastor, this second pastor would have a *Hilfsamt*, or auxiliary office, assisting his brother pastor. "Associate pastor," however, would have been a better term. If the second person called was a teacher, the congregation would create a new position, which would be a branch or form of the public ministry. The congregation now had called the teacher to perform certain functions of the parish ministry as a *Hilfsamt* that were formerly assigned to the pastor and embraced his office. The teacher, however, did not work for the pastor. He worked for the congregation with the pastor in a particular field.[47]

Mueller concluded his analysis of Thesis VIII by postulating:

> Even though we can justify Walther's use of the term "auxiliary office," it is evident that the term has tended to confuse. It has been employed to designate the position of teaching as a branch of the pastorate and, hence, subordinate to the pastorate. Actually the position of teacher is not a branch of the pastorate, nor is it subordinate to the pastorate, but like the pastorate it is one of the branches or forms of the general ministry. To avoid confusion, we ought to discard the term "auxiliary office" altogether and speak only of the position of teacher, likewise of the position of pastor.[48]

Mueller attempted to summarize what he considered to be Walther's position: Christians, organized into congregations, exercising their God-given prerogative, create whatever positions they deem necessary for the adequate dis-

---

[46] Mueller, *The Ministry of the Lutheran Teacher*, 92–93.

[47] Mueller, *The Ministry of the Lutheran Teacher*, 93–94.

[48] Mueller, *The Ministry of the Lutheran Teacher*, 94–95.

charge of the ministry in their midst. Although created by human beings, these positions are a divine institution because they are branches or positions of the one divinely instituted office of the ministry, the *ministerium ecclesiae*, which was instituted by Christ. The call given to the incumbents determines the functions of their ministries. The preparation of children for the fulfillment of their priestly and stewardship duties belongs to the performance of the ministry. Such preparation includes the teaching of the secular branches; hence the teaching of the secular branches is embraced in the call the congregation extends to a teacher[49] because, strictly speaking, the distinction between the sacred and the secular does not exist for Christians.[50]

In reference to women teachers, Mueller stated that "Sunday school teachers, Bible class teachers, and women teachers in our schools, all have a divine call. Of course, their responsibility is far more restricted than that of a pastor or a male teacher in the school."[51] According to Mueller,

> Even before the fall, God ordained that the man should be the head of the woman and that the woman should be subject to the man. After the fall the Lord ordained that the man should rule over the woman. According to the Law, woman is to occupy a subordinate position to man, a position which is quite consistent with love.
>
> ... On the authority of the Old Testament Scriptures [1 Cor. 14:34 and 1 Tim. 2:11-15] he [Paul] teaches that women must remain silent at such public gatherings composed of men and women. A woman who would violate that rule would be guilty of exercising authority over man. Paul enjoins silence upon women in situations of this kind.[52]

Mueller, however, refused to be identified with the view that women do not have a call to teach regardless of circumstances. For Mueller, Scripture does not absolutely forbid women to teach. Nowhere are they forbidden to teach children, nor are they forbidden to teach in behalf of the congregation. Mueller felt that what Paul forbids is for women to appear before public gatherings of the church as teachers, to speak at the meetings of the congregation, and to teach men. Such would be inconsistent with the nature of women and their natural relationship to men.[53]

Writing in the early 1960s, Mueller's view at that time was

---

[49] Mueller, *The Ministry of the Lutheran Teacher*, 137–138.

[50] Mueller, *The Ministry of the Lutheran Teacher*, 147.

[51] Mueller, *The Ministry of the Lutheran Teacher*, 163–164.

[52] Mueller, *The Ministry of the Lutheran Teacher*, 164.

[53] Mueller, *The Ministry of the Lutheran Teacher*, 163–166.

Our church ... makes a distinction between male teachers and women teachers because of the peculiar functions for which God has designed the man and the woman. Male teachers enter the service of the church with the intention of continuing in office until the Lord relieves them of their duties, something not required of women. Marriage does not interfere with the faithful performance of the task of the male teacher. Moreover, he is free from the restrictions God's Word has imposed on the woman. He may take an active part in the voters' meetings; he may have charge of the service in the absence of the pastor; and he may perform other functions, including the so-called sacerdotal functions, at the behest of the congregation. This wider field of activity, indeed, does not affect the status of the male teacher.[54]

Mueller believed that the "Solemn Agreement" in the appointment of women teachers took these principles into account. God made woman for the sacred function of motherhood and to be a helpmeet for man. Women were called into the ministry of teaching with the understanding that they were free at any time to withdraw from the classroom and marry.[55]

STEPHEN A. SCHMIDT

In 1972 the Lutheran Education Association published the polemical book *Powerless Pedagogues*, by Stephen A. Schmidt, professor of education at Concordia Teachers College, River Forest, Illinois. In this work Schmidt held that, from the time of the formation of the Synod, a lack of theological clarity concerning the status of teachers existed. Teachers were almost clergy, yet almost laypersons. Their theological status remained unclear throughout the history of the Synod. This lack of clarity, Schmidt believed, was intentional, for it tended to keep teachers in their places, auxiliary to the ordained clergy.[56]

In Schmidt's view, after the teachers seminary was separated from the theological seminary, the standards and education of the teachers seminary were seriously impaired. After this time, the length of the educational preparation for the preaching ministry exceeded that of the teaching ministry, and, as a result, the pastor became far better educated and more knowledgeable than the Lutheran teacher. At the teachers' institutions, according to Schmidt, the education of teachers has consistently been a process of paternalistic indoctrination. Early professors at the Addison Teachers Seminary were all members of the pastoral clergy. The first teacher was employed there as a professor only after the seminary was ten years old. The majority of the faculty were educated as pastors during the first fifty years of the Synod's history. It was Schmidt's belief that, through a careful process, teachers were taught their proper place in the public ministry.

---

54 Mueller, *The Ministry of the Lutheran Teacher*, 166.

55 Mueller, *The Ministry of the Lutheran Teacher*, 167.

56 Schmidt, *Powerless Pedagogues*, 5.

They were taught to remain subservient to the office of the pastor, both in the educational institutions for teachers as well as in the professional literature of the Synod.[57] In addition, according to Schmidt, the role of the teacher in the life of the church was not clearly defined and, as a result, teachers were unsure of the precise nature of their ministries. This uncertainty led to a weakened professional self-image. Unsure of his office and lacking consistent ecclesiastical identity, the teacher had to compensate with over-dedication, proving again and again his superlative service and dedicated humility. He had to work harder than others to vindicate his worth and justify his being and, in some cases, his job.[58]

As Schmidt observed, early teachers were often pastors, and those who began as teachers often transferred into the preaching ministry later in their careers. Teaching was then an apprenticeship to the preaching ministry. As more non-pastors filled the classrooms of the parochial schools, difficulties arose, especially where two or more teachers were called to a single parish. The pastor then became the dominant figure in the public ministry of the parish, while the teacher assumed a lesser status. Pastors were careful to define that role, and as teachers multiplied in numbers, the talk of their humble servanthood and lower position became more prolific. The teachers' lack of self-esteem was structured into their service. Teachers were in the classroom much of the day, living out a large portion of their adult lives with children. The humble tasks of the parish ministry fell to the teacher. He continued to accept these tasks as an obedient servant. Corporately, teachers developed a passivity, accepting duty and responsibility, but rarely initiating leadership in the parish or in the church at large.[59]

In Schmidt's view, one might lay the responsibility for the lack of professional self-worth at the doorstep of the Lutheran pastor. Surely in many cases he contributed by his paternalism and use of pious theological jargon to insure obedience and loyal servanthood. The incessant reminders from the clergy that the teaching office was "lower," "less than," "under," and "auxiliary to" the pastor's "more holy office," the "highest office," could only undermine the professional dignity of the teacher. Schmidt also stated that the local parish contributed to the gradual deterioration of teacher pride. Often overlooked and subjected to meaningless tasks, the teacher lost his professional zest. However, Schmidt believed that the ultimate responsibility for the profession's low esteem rested with the profession itself. The teaching ministry had been its own worst enemy. Through inactivity and subordination of teachers in both district and Synod work, teachers often found themselves choosing to sit on the sidelines, quietly insisting that their superiors, clergy and laity, continue to conduct the affairs of

---

[57] Schmidt, *Powerless Pedagogues*, 5.

[58] Schmidt, *Powerless Pedagogues*, 60.

[59] Schmidt, *Powerless Pedagogues*, 61–62.

the Synod. They became enslaved by parish definition, pastoral paternalism, and personal frustration.[60]

It was Schmidt's interpretation that the constant shortage of teachers led congregations to employ less than adequately educated teachers. The standards of admission into the teaching ministry were lowered by individual congregations and corporately by the Synod. Teachers were called into service without completing their courses of study. During the last decade of the nineteenth century public school teachers began to earn more than their parochial counterparts. Since 1900 Lutheran teachers' salaries have been embarrassingly inadequate. Teachers have always tended to accept this condition as a symbol of their commitment and dedication.[61]

Finally, according to Schmidt, teachers were often the bearers of an inferiority illness, birthed in a lack of ecclesiastical identity and nurtured by decades of careful coaching by the masters of theological gamesmanship. The clergy maintained power by appeal to the theological. The laymen maintained power with pocketbook strength. The teacher was left powerless, deserted by his colleagues, disillusioned by his history, and taught by the clergy that he was inferior. The clergy knew the rules of the power game in the church and carefully guarded the lay-clergy balance. The powerless pedagogue chose to remain powerless.[62]

THE CTCR REAFFIRMS WALTHER'S AND THE SYNOD'S POSITION ON THE MINISTRY

In response to a number of requests for clarification of the teacher's role within the Synod, in 1981 the Synod's Commission on Theology and Church Relations (CTCR) restated the synodical position that the pastoral office is the highest ministerial position and that all other church ministries are auxiliary to it. This reaffirmation, coming on the heels of seven years of research, was published as a report of the CTCR and titled "The Ministry: Offices, Procedures, and Nomenclature."[63] The commission did not refer to the work of Stellhorn, Mueller, or Schmidt in its official final report.

According to the Reverend Dr. Samuel H. Nafzger, executive secretary of the CTCR,

> the Commission began its study on "The Ministry" by conducting a thorough exegetical study of what the Scriptures have to say about the ministry. It then studied what the Lutheran Confessions have to say about this doc-

---

[60] Schmidt, *Powerless Pedagogues*, 61–63.

[61] Schmidt, *Powerless Pedagogues*, 78–79.

[62] Schmidt, *Powerless Pedagogues*, 89.

[63] Report of the Commission on Theology and Church Relations, 4–5.

trine. It also reviewed the writings of the orthodox theologians on this topic, as well as those of the fathers in the Missouri Synod, contemporary theologians in this country and other countries, especially in Northern Europe. After four years of researching and studying this assignment, the Commission discussed a lengthy and rather technical draft of this report with the faculties of the Synod's two seminaries, with representatives of the Synod's teachers colleges, with synodical staff people from the Board of Higher Education, the Board of Parish Education, the personnel and statistical department, and finally with Synod's legal counsel. On at least three different occasions this report was discussed with the Council of Presidents. Following these consultations, the original draft was completely re-written, then discussed and revised by the plenary CTCR, and finally published and distributed to the Synod for study and guidance in October, 1981.[64]

It was the perspective of the CTCR that the

> Office of the Public Ministry ... is the divinely established office referred to in Scripture as "shepherd," "elder," or "overseer." This term is equivalent to "the pastoral office." Within this office are contained all the functions of the ministry of the Word and sacrament in the church.

> Auxiliary Offices ... are offices established by the church. Those who are called to serve in them are authorized to perform certain of the function(s) of the office of the public ministry. These offices are "ministry" and they are "public," yet they are not the office of the public ministry. Rather, they are auxiliary to that unique pastoral office, and those who hold these offices perform their assigned functions under the supervision of the holders of the pastoral office. Such offices are established by the church as the need arises, and their specific functions are determined by the church. The most common auxiliary office today is the office of the teaching ministry.[65]

According to the CTCR,

> the church has the right to distinguish such auxiliary offices of the church from each other. Some require extensive knowledge of Scripture, ability to teach or to counsel, or other capabilities that are closely related to the teaching and shepherding functions of the office of the public ministry. The church has always exercised the right to designate some of its offices as so involved in the spiritual functions of the office of the public ministry that it has provided specific training, is more formal in summoning members of the church to such offices and has rightly included such offices within its concept of "ministry." Such offices call for functions that not only are necessary for the functioning of the public ministry but that only the church performs as an institution. Thus, the teaching of the faith in a Christian school is a

---

[64] Nafzger, "The CTCR's Report on 'The Ministry'," 143–144.

[65] Report of the Commission on Theology and Church Relations, 12.

function unique to the church. Properly speaking, a professional, trained teacher who is called as a teacher by the church may be said to be performing a function of the office of the public ministry. The teaching of the faith to the children and youth of the flock is a major duty of the pastoral office. To refer to it as "the teaching ministry" is less awkward and readily understandable in the church.

By using the term "teaching ministry" we are indicating the special nature of the auxiliary office of teacher in our church. One who is in the "teaching ministry" (man or woman) meets the following qualifications, established by the church. He or she

- has been trained in the educational institutions of the church, has received specific training in the understanding and teaching of religion, and has been certified as suitable and eligible for the teaching ministry by a faculty of the church. In some cases the requirements have been met by means of a colloquy program that includes training and evaluation.

- has been placed into the teaching ministry formally and officially by an assignment of the Board of Assignments, which is the Council of Presidents of the Synod.

- is given authority to function in the teaching ministry in specific places by the formal call of a congregation or other legitimate calling agency (e.g., a District, the Synod, or others).

- serves under the supervision of the called pastor in a congregation or under other pastoral supervision in nonparish calls.

- does work that is specifically spiritual in nature. Although he/she may teach some "secular" subjects, the philosophy of Lutheran education includes the demand that the faith of the church be evident in all activities of the school. Law and Gospel, sin and grace are operative in the curriculum and methodology of a Lutheran school.

- knows and publicly subscribes to the Lutheran Confessions.

- is accepted formally as a member of the Synod, with the obligation to attend official conferences and district conventions.

- may be chosen to represent groups of teachers as a delegate to conventions of the Synod.

- is answerable for the confessional purity of his/her teaching and is pledged to a life that befits the Gospel of Jesus Christ.

- may be removed from office because of impure doctrine, an ungodly life, or incompetence.

- is pledged to be concerned for the spiritual and eternal welfare of those committed to his/her care.

Although not pledged to remain in the teaching office for a lifetime, the normal expectancy of the church and of teacher candidates is that, unless prevented by personal circumstances, the teaching ministry of an individual will be followed as a lifelong calling.[66]

The CTCR believed that the pastoral office is unique in that all the functions of the church's ministry belong to it. There is only one pastoral office, but the office which is referred to as "the office of the public ministry" has multiple functions, some of which are best handled by another person. The parochial school teacher, thus, performs the teaching function of the pastoral office.[67]

In the view of the CTCR, a Christian teacher is not merely a Christian who teaches, but a servant of Christ and the church who, at the call of the church, is helping the called pastor to fulfill his mandate to teach the Gospel.

> The congregation is blessed when it places at the side of its pastor faithful and capable teachers, for instance, who enhance his administration of the office of public ministry. Their office is a public office and an office of ministry, although it is not the office of the public ministry of Word and sacrament, that is, the pastoral office … . The teaching office in the church is auxiliary to the … pastoral ministry. It is grounded not merely in the priesthood of believers but, through the office of the public ministry, in the ministry of Christ and the apostles. The fact that not all appreciate this idea does not change its tremendous theological significance for all who labor in the church. To ground the auxiliary offices of the church in a vague and unembodied "ministry in general" is no gain for anyone. To see them flow from the specific office that is amply attested and exemplified in the New Testament and strongly championed in the Lutheran Confessions is a higher view of the auxiliary offices than that which would seek an independent grounding separate from the office of the public ministry of Word and sacrament.[68]

The CTCR concluded by saying that all who serve in the pastoral ministry or its auxiliary offices must be called by the church. Those who are "called" come under the supervision of the whole church.[69] Since 1981, synodical policies on and definitions of ministry have been based on the CTCR report.

Summing Up

There is historical precedent within the Missouri Synod for its position that the teaching ministry is an auxiliary ministry. The precedent began with Walther

---

[66] Report of the Commission on Theology and Church Relations, 17–19.

[67] Report of the Commission on Theology and Church Relations, 19.

[68] Report of the Commission on Theology and Church Relations, 27–28.

[69] Report of the Commission on Theology and Church Relations, 37–38.

in 1851 and was reaffirmed by the CTCR report on "The Ministry: Offices, Procedures, and Nomenclature" in 1981.

The scriptural and confessional precedent for an auxiliary teaching ministry, however, appears to have led to some controversy. Mueller, especially, and Stellhorn have contended that there is scriptural warrant for a general ministry with many branches. That the pastoral ministry is the highest general ministry with all other ministries as auxiliary to it, as the Synod has stated as its official position, of course, is contested by these sources.

From the prospective teaching minister's point of view, the work of ministry continues regardless of how the issue is defined. Officially and in practice, however, the teaching ministry remains an auxiliary office to the pastoral ministry. The Lutheran teacher does not hold the office of public ministry, at least not in the fullest sense, yet is considered to be part of the ministerium of The Lutheran Church—Missouri Synod.

DISCUSSION TOPICS AND SUGGESTED PROJECTS

1. In your opinion, in what sense is the Lutheran school teacher a minister?

2. How might the question of the Lutheran school teacher as minister be analyzed from the perspective of the pastoral clergy? From the perspective of teachers? From the perspective of the laity?

3. One might argue that the CTCR's 1981 report effectively thwarts women from entering the pastoral ministry of the Missouri Synod. Analyze the Commission's position regarding the auxiliary ministry of the teacher over against the emerging role of women in society.

4. Arrange an in-class panel discussion with theology professors at your university that hold the "mediating school" and "functional school" perspectives on the doctrine of the ministry. Ask them to discuss why they adhere to the positions they hold.

5. What does this controversy determine regarding your personal service to the Lord?

6. Cite instances where this issue remains controversial within The Lutheran Church—Missouri Synod.

RESOURCES, INFLUENCES, AND SUGGESTED FURTHER READING

Beck, Walter H. *Lutheran Elementary Schools in the United States: A History of the Development of Parochial Schools and Synodical Educational Policies and Programs.* St. Louis: Concordia Publishing House, 1939.

Dallmann, Wm., et al., eds. *Walther and the Church*. St. Louis: Concordia Publishing House, 1938.

Hilgendorf, Mary. "C. F. W. Walther and Education in The Lutheran Church—Missouri Synod." *Lutheran Education* 135 (September–October 1999, November–December 1999, and January–February 2000): 21–26, 90–94, and 143–150.

Kohn, W. C. "Christian Day Schools of the Lutheran Church." *Lutheran School Journal* 54 (January 1919): 8–14.

Mueller, Arnold C. *The Ministry of the Lutheran Teacher: A Study to Determine the Position of the Lutheran Parish School Teacher within the Public Ministry of the Church*. St. Louis: Concordia Publishing House, 1964.

Nafzger, Samuel H. "The CTCR's Report on 'The Ministry.'" *Lutheran Education* 118 (January–February 1983): 132–157.

Report of the Commission on Theology and Church Relations. "The Ministry: Offices, Procedures, and Nomenclature." St. Louis: The Lutheran Church—Missouri Synod, September 1981.

Rietschel, William C. "An Analysis of the Educational Ideas of August C. Stellhorn, 1921–1963." Ed.D. diss., Loyola University of Chicago, 1980.

Schmidt, Stephen A. *Powerless Pedagogues: An Interpretative Essay on the History of the Lutheran Teacher in the Missouri Synod. Twenty-Ninth Yearbook of the Lutheran Education Association*. River Forest, Ill.: Lutheran Education Association, 1972.

Stellhorn, August C. "The Lutheran Teacher in the Ministry of the Church." Address to the Western District Teachers Conference in St. Louis, 13 October 1952. Concordia Historical Institute, St. Louis. Mimeographed.

————. "The Lutheran Teacher's Position in the Ministry of the Congregation." Address to the Missouri Synod Educational Conference in Seward, Nebraska, July 1949. Concordia Historical Institute, St. Louis. Mimeographed.

————. *Schools of The Lutheran Church—Missouri Synod*. St. Louis: Concordia Publishing House, 1963.

————. "The Woman Teacher's Call—An Explanation." *Board for Parish Education Bulletin* (November 1954): 5.

Toepper, Robert M. "Is the Lutheran Teacher a Minister? Yes, But … . The Question of Teacher Ministry in Historical Perspective." *Lutheran Education* 131 (November–December 1995, January–February 1996, and May–June 1996): 62–79, 124–142, and 249–268.

Walther, C. F. W. *Church and Ministry* (Kirche und Amt): *Witness of the Evangelical Lutheran Church on the Question of the Church and the Ministry*. Translated by J. T. Mueller. St. Louis: Concordia Publishing House, 1987.

————. "Does a Professor of a Church College Have a Divine Call?" Sermon delivered at the installation of the Director and Assistant Rector of Concordia College in St. Louis, 31 March 1856. Translated by A. C. Stellhorn. Concordia Historical Institute, St. Louis. Mimeographed.

6

THE LUTHERAN TEACHER
AS A PROFESSIONAL

This chapter segues from the theoretical to the practical. The prospective Lutheran school teacher needs to have a basic understanding of such matters as status, supply and demand of various ministry opportunities, salary, preparation, and placement for service. In addition, he or she should be guided into a realistic, yet positive, view of the teaching office within the Missouri Synod. To that end, we conclude this chapter with an exploration of issues related to satisfaction with the teaching ministry as well as personal and professional development opportunities available to uplift those in service.

STATUS AND SUPPLY OF LUTHERAN TEACHERS

Two major factors that apparently influence social status in our society are one's occupational standing and salary level. These factors, in turn, are affected by supply and demand. When the supply of individuals in an occupation surpasses demand, their standing and salaries exhibit a tendency to decline. This leads to diminishing social status. On the other hand, when demand exceeds supply, salaries, standing, and social status tend to increase. Whether any of this is applicable to Lutheran school teachers is, of course, arguable.

OCCUPATIONAL STANDING

In the broader social context, one's occupational standing refers to the respect a particular society has for a line of work. Generally, those occupations perceived as making an especially valuable contribution to society possess high standing. Those pursuits requiring considerable education or skill and limited manual or physical labor also tend toward high standing. Historically, the vocational calling of elementary and secondary teacher ranked relatively high relating to societal respect.

These aspects notwithstanding, the previous chapter assures one considering teaching in a Lutheran school that he or she certainly has standing within the ministerium of The Lutheran Church—Missouri Synod. However, as was also explored in chapter 5, there is some disagreement as to that standing. There is no disagreement, however, about the Lutheran teaching minister's valuable contribution to the work of the kingdom.

Salary

Although traditionally teachers have enjoyed a relatively high occupational standing, they received relatively low salaries. An argument can be made that salaries reflect the current values inherent in the American social order. If this is true and teachers are making an especially valuable contribution to society, how can society reasonably compensate teachers with low salaries?

The same can be asked of the Missouri Synod. If the Lutheran teacher's ministry to children and adolescents is an especially valuable contribution to God's kingdom, how can the church reasonably compensate Lutheran teachers at low levels? For example, the average starting salary for a first-year Lutheran elementary teacher placed during the 1998–99 placement year was slightly more than $22,000. By way of comparison, beginning Catholic elementary lay teachers earned an average salary of only $17,683 two years previously (1996–97).[1] The average salary for a first-year Lutheran secondary teacher placed during 1998–99 was only negligibly higher than their Lutheran elementary counterpart at $22,219.[2]

While compensation for teaching varies considerably among and within synodical Districts for both first-year and experienced Lutheran teachers, one is not especially encouraged when the average salaries for all full-time elementary or secondary teachers are perused. Full-time Lutheran elementary teachers with a bachelor's degree received an average salary of $24,641 in 1998–99; for those with a master's degree the figure rose to $31,743. Two years previously, the salary figure for Catholic elementary lay teachers with a bachelor's degree and higher degrees was $21,882.[3] At the secondary level in 1998–99 the Lutheran teacher with a bachelor's degree received $24,899 and with a master's degree $34,146 for his or her service.[4] One should not overlook that Lutheran teachers usually receive an excellent benefit package through the Synod's Worker Benefit Plans (Concordia Health Plan, Concordia Disability and Survivor Plan, and Concordia Retirement Plan); yet, a person who is considering service in the Lutheran teaching ministry needs to understand that salaries are problematic and, as will be addressed later in this chapter, can contribute to decreased satisfaction with one's ministry and also to eventual attrition from the teaching ministry.

---

[1] Data made available by Sister Dale McDonald of the National Catholic Education Association, February 22, 2000.

[2] "Commissioned Ministers of Religion: 1998-99 Placement Statistics" (St. Louis: Board for Higher Education, The Lutheran Church—Missouri Synod, 1999), 1–10.

[3] Data made available by Sister Dale McDonald of the National Catholic Education Association, February 22, 2000.

[4] Ross E. Stueber, ed., "1998-99 Statistical Report Summary, Schools and Early Childhood Centers of The Lutheran Church—Missouri Synod" (St. Louis: Department of School Ministry, The Lutheran Church—Missouri Synod, 1999), 10.

It is also important to point out that The Lutheran Church—Missouri Synod and its various Districts are attempting to address the issue of substandard salaries. Each District has salary guidelines and District presidents will refuse to sign call documents if salaries fall below suggested guidelines. The Synod's Department of School Ministry recommends that salaries should be in line with local public schools. Ultimately, tuition may be the key. The Department of School Ministry has reached the conclusion that tuition-driven Lutheran schools tend to pay higher salaries. What appears to evolve is that tuition rates established by congregational school boards result in planned salary increases as opposed to salaries that evolve from whatever remains as surplus after all other expenditures have been addressed.[5]

SUPPLY AND DEMAND

On the national level, many analysts predict a shortage of teachers for the next ten or fifteen years. Others argue that there will not be a major shortage in the next several years.

Given the arguments on both sides of the issue, predicting teacher supply and demand is difficult at best. In chapter 9, we prognosticate that there will be a shortage of good teachers in this new millennium generally and, more specifically, that there will be fewer synodically certified teachers available for ministry in Lutheran schools because of the lower numbers in synodical universities preparing for the teaching ministry.

Of course, those serving in teacher placement capacities know that awareness of a general demand for teachers is not as helpful as understanding the demands in specific educational fields. Nationally, such "special-needs" fields as special education, science, mathematics, and foreign languages will likely continue to have a shortage of competent teachers.

A recent survey of the teachers needs as perceived by synodical teacher placement officers, while not "scientific," may be instructive. Those who responded to this survey perceived computer-science education, early childhood education, elementary education (all levels), mathematics, music, science, and Spanish to be the teaching fields that are, and will continue to be for some time, in the greatest demand in Lutheran schools.

Respondents were also asked to comment on the factors that influence supply and demand. Candidate mobility and indebtedness were noted as being among the most significant influences.[6]

---

[5] Information made available by Carl Moser, Director of the Department of School Ministry, The Lutheran Church—Missouri Synod, February 22, 2000.

[6] O. John Zillman, "Lutheran Teacher Supply and Demand" (Unpublished survey, Office of Educational and Synodical Placement, Concordia University, River Forest, Ill., August 1999).

Preparation of the Lutheran Teacher

Historically, if you could read, write, spell, and possessed good moral character, you could teach. Today, except for alternative certification or temporary certification, all states require a bachelor's degree or five years of college work, with satisfactory completion of certain educational courses, for entrance into teaching.

Preservice Lutheran Teacher Preparation

The preparation of Lutheran teachers typically is organized around four principal elements: 1) General (or liberal) studies, 2) specialized subject field studies, 3) professional studies, and 4) theological studies. A *general* program combines the liberal arts and sciences and endeavors to provide the student with a broad cultural perspective. In general, *liberal* means to liberate, i.e., to free, the mind. The *specialized subject field* constitutes a concentration of courses in a specific subject area and furnishes the prospective Lutheran teacher with in-depth preparation for his or her chosen teaching field. This subject field is typically called the student's "major" or "minor" among the various colleges and universities in the Concordia University System. Lutheran secondary teachers, because they are as a rule certified in one subject field, commonly complete a greater amount of course work in one or two areas. Lutheran elementary teachers are responsible for many fields, but may also concentrate in areas such as the sciences, mathematics, music, art, physical education, and foreign language. *Professional education* is made up of course work intended to provide skills and a knowledge base regarding the art and science of teaching coupled with an understanding of the historical, philosophical, social, political, economic, legal, and cultural foundations of both Lutheran and public education. The study of *theology* for the Lutheran teacher is essential because it provides an understanding of Holy Scripture and the Lutheran Confessions and the teachings that undergird a Lutheran worldview.

There appears to be widespread agreement among Lutheran educators that the preparation of effective teaching ministers rests on these four components. However, differences of opinion exist regarding how much emphasis each element should receive in the preservice Lutheran teacher program of preparation. While no one argues the necessity of a solid theological underpinning, questions have arisen regarding how much time should be devoted to general-studies course work over against specialized subject fields and professional studies. There are also differing viewpoints concerning the extent to which practice in actual school settings, i.e., clinical experience, should be included in professional education courses.

Because synodical colleges and universities exist under differing state requirements, there is variance in credit requirements. Nationally, it is commonplace to require approximately 25 semester hours of professional course work for elementary teacher candidates and 20 hours for secondary candidates. Typically, education courses are distributed throughout the four-year program, but some institutions concentrate them during the last year. Still others may have a five-year program.

CERTIFICATION

The prospective Lutheran teacher needs to be cognizant of three types of certification that will or may impact their eventual service in the teaching ministry of the church: state, synodical, and colloquy. A brief review of each follows.

1. *State Teacher Certification*

Prospective Lutheran teachers may be required to be certified at the grade level or in the subject area they wish to teach in order to teach in some states, e.g., Michigan, Nebraska. However, many states leave it to the individual Lutheran schools

> to determine whether or not they wish to require certification. Others have provisions that make it possible for schools to have a percentage of teachers on their staffs who do not meet certification standards. Many also make it possible for teachers to begin teaching even when they do not meet all standards by issuing a certificate that specifies a time period to remove deficiencies.[7]

Although there is no "official Lutheran position" for or against certifying teachers, "[t]he church body strongly encourages its teachers to meet ... legal standards for the role."[8] Also, an ever-increasing number of Lutheran schools believe it is imperative for their teachers to hold state certification, even where they have the option not to require it. However, whether one is required to become state certified or not, it is good to remember that

> many heartaches would be avoided if every teacher ... would get at least one state certificate upon graduation and then keep a certificate in force at all times.

> Too many have a short range view. A new graduate who has a call to a school that does not require its faculty to have a certificate, in a state that gives [Lutheran] schools the option of requiring or not requiring a certificate for employment, often chooses not to pay the fee and take the trouble to complete the application process.[9]

A Lutheran teacher should procure a state teaching certificate for several reasons. One is that he or she "will not be spending their lifetimes in one school or state." Having a certificate in one state will facilitate the certification process in

---

[7] Glenn C. Einspahr, "State Certification Trends," *Lutheran Education* 119 (November–December 1983), 111.

[8] Lee Holtzen, "What Are We Teaching About the Call? Some Basic Concepts," in *The Call of the Lutheran Educator* (ed. Carl Moser; St. Louis: School Ministry Department, The Lutheran Church—Missouri Synod, n.d.), 14.

[9] Einspahr, "State Certification Trends," 111–112.

another state. Many states "will give a teacher a certificate that is equivalent to the one in force."[10] Also, circumstances may lead one to desire to teach in a public school. In such a case an advantage in having

> a valid state teaching certificate is that the number of years [the individual has] been [in possession] of a certificate is a matter of record. Often, it is necessary for a teacher to have an initial teaching certificate before [he or] she is eligible to receive the next higher level certificate.[11]

Finally,

> It is a good selling point for the Lutheran school when parents can be assured that its teachers have the same credentials as those who serve in the community's public schools. There is also the intangible value of psychological pride on the part of the teacher who is able to display a valid teaching certificate.[12]

Perhaps one of the most annoying problems in education is that certification requirements vary so widely from state to state. The reader is strongly encouraged to keep abreast of these variances as well as the frequent changes that occur in state teacher certification requirements.[13]

2. Synodical Certification

In order for teachers in a Lutheran school to be eligible for individual membership in The Lutheran Church—Missouri Synod, they must be designated as "ministers of religion—commissioned."[14] In a sense, to be so designated a prospective Lutheran teacher is subject to another certification process, somewhat more amorphous when compared to the very specific requirements for state teacher certification. As stated in Bylaw 2.09 of the Synodical Handbook, to be eligible for individual membership in the Synod and thereby be eligible to receive an initial and subsequent calls as a minister of the Gospel,

> A graduate of an authorized synodical institution must be declared qualified … and recommended by the faculty of the respective synodical institution . … Candidates who may be declared qualified … are those who … will have satisfactorily completed the prescribed courses of studies and will have received diplomas from their respective institutions. … In addition, they must have indicated complete dedication to the ministry and evidenced a

---

[10] Einspahr, "State Certification Trends," 112.

[11] Einspahr, "State Certification Trends," 112.

[12] Einspahr, "State Certification Trends," 112–113.

[13] One of the more helpful resources available for this task is John Tryneski, ed., *Requirements for Certification* (64th ed.; Chicago: University of Chicago Press, 1999–2000).

[14] *Handbook of The Lutheran Church—Missouri Synod: 1998 Edition* (St. Louis: The Lutheran Church—Missouri Synod, 1998), 23. New editions of the Handbook appear following each synodical convention, incorporating the changes approved by that convention.

readiness for service in the church. Finally, to be declared qualified and recommended by the faculties ... for their specific types of service in the
church, the appropriate faculty ... must be satisfied that the individual will
meet all personal, professional, and the theological requirements of those
who hold the office of ministry. ...[15]

How the above requirement is implemented will vary according to each synodical teacher preparation program. Also, upon being certified for the teaching
ministry by the respective synodical institution of higher education, one typically receives a Lutheran Teacher Diploma signifying that he or she has met the
Synod's eligibility requirements in addition to a degree or academic diploma.

3. *Certification by Colloquy*

The Synod has developed a system of preparation and set requirements that
permit those who have not graduated from one of its colleges or universities to
enter into the teaching ministry. This is known as the Teacher Colloquy Program
and is designed to assist college graduates who have been approved by their
District president and representatives of the Synodical Committee on Colloquies
to qualify for this important service to the church.

The Synod's Committee on Colloquies for the Teaching Ministry has been
established to direct synodical activity in matters pertaining to teacher colloquies. This committee, consisting of the first vice-president of the Synod and two of
the presidents of synodical colleges or universities offering a bachelor's degree in
teacher education, is responsible for the establishment of academic and theological standards for admission to the teaching ministry by colloquy.

As already indicated, all states, as well as national and regional accrediting
agencies, have established requirements for certification of teachers. The synodical colleges and universities attempt to prepare their students to meet those
requirements. The church generally considers it important that all teachers
placed by the church also should meet these certification requirements.
Therefore, the requirements of the teacher colloquy program for persons who
seek to teach in Lutheran schools are comparable to those made of public school
teachers certified by the various states.

Specifically, the colloquy applicant must meet the following requirements or
their equivalent:

- Be at least 25 years of age.

- Have completed a college or university program culminating in a bachelor's degree.

- Possess state certification as a teacher or qualify for a teaching certificate
  as part of the Teacher Colloquy Program.

---

[15] *Handbook of The Lutheran Church—Missouri Synod: 1998 Edition*, 23–24.

- The satisfactory completion of certain required courses or their equivalent in biblical interpretation of the Old and New Testaments, Lutheran doctrine, church history and practice, and religious education so as to meet the academic and theological standards established by the Colloquy Committee of Synod, of which courses a minimum of four regular program courses must be taken with the faculty of a synodical college offering a bachelor's degree in teacher education.

- Student teaching under the supervision of a synodical college offering a bachelor's degree in teacher education or one year of successful teaching in a school recognized by the Missouri Synod.

In order to meet these requirements, the college or university responsible for the individual's colloquy experience organizes a program of study that includes the following specific requirements or their equivalent:

- About fifteen semester or twenty quarter-hours of biblical studies (including doctrine).

- About nine semester or twelve quarter-hours of church history, church ethics, and Christian education.

- Courses, readings, or other measurable experiences in the psychology of learning and methods of teaching, according to need.

The above requirements can be met by comprehensive examinations in each of the fields listed. However, formal course work is the preferred route.

Official statements regarding the Teacher Colloquy Program of the Synod are included in the Synodical Handbook. Specifically, Bylaws 6.105 through 6.121 (1998 edition) address admission to the teaching ministry via colloquy.[16]

Synodical Placement Process: Past and Present

Change is an inevitable process of the movement of time and perhaps nowhere more applicable than in describing placement procedures for candidates in their "first calls" into the educational ministries of The Lutheran Church—Missouri Synod. Because of the periodic discussion surrounding teacher placement procedures and the importance of prospective Lutheran teachers understanding the process, this section of the chapter attempts to explain and evaluate those dynamics much more extensively than it has treated several of the previous topics included in this chapter.

When the author graduated from then Concordia Teachers College, River Forest, Illinois, in 1965, he had been assigned his first call into the teaching min-

---

[16] *Handbook of The Lutheran Church—Missouri Synod: 1998 Edition*, 115–118.

istry by the Synod's Council of Presidents (COP), which he was expected to accept. Acceptance was contingent upon completion of his program with satisfactory academic and personal records. The assignment was initiated by the congregation when it resolved to call a teacher from the graduate pool and submitted call documents to its District president. The latter then studied it, compiled and signed it with others submitted to his District, and forwarded them prior to mid-March with an accompanying letter to the Synod's secretary of schools in St. Louis.

The secretary of school's office then classified, summarized, abstracted, and assigned a number to each call document. Copies of the call documents were then sent to the college placement directors (River Forest, St. Paul, and Seward at the time) for perusal in preparation for the official spring assignment meeting in St. Louis. The placement director, who had his candidates' backgrounds, skills, aptitudes, and weaknesses, then tentatively matched his candidates to appropriate calls.

Certainly, the focal point of this process was the spring convening in St. Louis of the placement committee from each of the then terminal synodical institutions with a teacher education program. Typically this committee was composed of the college president, dean of students, and placement director. Through discussion, reconsideration, and adjustment among the placement directors (with input from their respective institutional committee members and also from each District's superintendent of schools or education executive), a tentative list of assignments was prepared and presented to the teacher placement subcommittee of the Council of Presidents.

When a consensus was reached between the college placement committees and the Council of Presidents' teacher placement subcommittee, another list was prepared and presented to a plenary meeting of the Council for final approval. However, before the final vote, the District president and/or his District's school superintendent or educational executive could, and often did, appear before the subcommittee and placement committees seeking explanation and/or requesting reconsideration regarding a call submitted from their District. Finally, a unanimous vote by the Council would then conclude its function as the Synod's Board of Assignments (BOA) and each District president would notify the calling bodies within their jurisdiction of the Council's action.

While the foregoing procedural precis points to a cumbersome process, e.g., the spring placement meeting in St. Louis typically required two to three weeks of sometimes intense sessions, it appeared to be a process appropriate to its time. If not, then perhaps those of the author's generation who experienced this process and who still look back upon it somewhat fondly have allowed nostalgia to cloud their perspective.

A number of factors have contributed to the ongoing redefinition of the initial placement process for the Synod's educational ministries.[17] The author would suggest that an apparent Vietnam War-induced candidate oversupply, stemming in part from the male teacher ministerial draft deferral, led calling bodies to ask for a greater choice in selecting a teacher from this oversupply in the candidate pool. This has led to calling bodies being more closely involved in the placement decision-making process. A natural offshoot has been that teacher placement candidates have successfully sought similar opportunity of choice and involvement in the process.

Essentially, what has currently evolved is a seven-step process that may eventually result in a "designated call" or "first-placement" into an initial educational ministry of the church.[18] Rather than submitting call documents to their respective District presidents, calling bodies now typically initiate contact with the placement directors of the synodical colleges and universities, specifying the qualifications for the position to be filled.

The placement director will review the institution's existing pool of candidates and provide the name(s) and a brief sketch of the candidate(s) deemed appropriate for consideration by the calling body. If requested, a credential containing pertinent biographical and professional information will also be sent for review by appropriately designated representatives of the prospective calling body. The candidate's name may be submitted for consideration to any number of calling bodies at the same time, usually three or four at any one time. Just because a calling body has the name of a candidate does not mean that they have reserved access.

The third step in the process is similar to a type of screening interview. Calling bodies will make contact, usually by telephone, with candidates whom they have deemed appropriate for possibly meeting their staffing needs, and provide them with basic information related to the position. The candidates, in turn, may ask preliminary questions and should indicate whether they are interested in being considered further.

Step four is the selection interview. Arrangements are made for a more formal telephone, on-site, or on-campus interview. Obviously, this step tends to be the pivotal one in the designation process, for it is at this juncture that the candidate(s) have the opportunity to perform "under fire," responding to questions ranging from why they chose to prepare for the Lutheran teaching ministry to

---

[17] See Lee Roy Holtzen and Roy C. Krause, "Teacher Placement in the LC-MS," in *The Role of the Lutheran Teacher* (8th ed.; Seward, Nebr.: Graphic Printing Company, 1997), 17–40; and William Lehmann, Jr., "New Directions in Teacher Placement," *Lutheran Education* 113 (September–October 1977), 32–35.

[18] See *Procedures for Calling Commissioned Ministers in The Lutheran Church—Missouri Synod* (St. Louis: The Board for Higher Education and Congregational Services, The Lutheran Church—Missouri Synod, 1999), 3–5.

how they would incorporate current pedagogical approaches into the instructional program. Prayerful, rational decision-making is, or at least should be, the next step in this process. After weighing the qualifications and responses of each of the candidates interviewed, those designated (e.g., call committee, personnel committee) to recommend to the authorized body (i.e., voters, board of directors, school board) should select that individual believed to be best qualified to meet their staffing needs.

However, before a formal resolution issuing a call is enacted, the selected candidate's placement director is informed. Functioning as a counselor, the placement director will ascertain if the selected candidate wishes to be designated by the calling body. If the candidate sees no obstacle to considering the call, other bodies looking at the candidate are requested to remove the candidate's name from consideration and the placement director also ceases sharing the candidate's name with any new contacts that might be received.

After formally resolving to designate their call to the specific candidate selected, the calling body, just as it did in the past, submits call documents to its District president. However, accompanying these documents is a letter to the Board of Assignments designating the selected candidate. The entire packet is then forwarded to the candidate's placement director, who provides a copy of pertinent information to the Synod's Board for Higher Education. Since the 1978–1979 placement year, the Board for Higher Education has had responsibility for classifying, summarizing, abstracting, and numbering first-placement calls for the Council of Presidents as it functions as the Board of Assignments. This, in essence, is the sixth of the seven steps in the current educational ministries placement process.

The final step is the unanimous vote of the Council of Presidents followed by notification by each District president that their District's calling bodies have, in fact, been assigned their predetermined designations. There is no longer a spring placement meeting. The Council of Presidents' approval occurs on a rolling basis at each of its regularly scheduled meetings.

As is apparent, historically the primary shift in this calling process is the heightened involvement of both candidate and calling body prior to formal assignment. Also apparent is the significantly diminished role of the Council of Presidents functioning as the Synod's Board of Assignments. The Synodical Handbook (1998 edition) still fixes responsibility for the assignment of graduates to the Council of Presidents. As stated in Bylaw 2.11:

- [T]he Council of Presidents, acting as the Board of Assignments, shall regularly assign to qualified graduates of synodical educational institutions and workers available from colloquy programs as "first calls" those calls that have been duly extended by authorized calling bodies (Bylaw 2.15) for ordained ministers and commissioned ministers if positions for which candidates are qualified are available.

- The placement officers of the respective institutions shall be consulted before the assignments are made.

- The President of the District in which a candidate is to be placed shall be consulted and his suggestions and recommendations shall be part of the final recommendation to the Board of Assignments.[19]

However, in practice, rather than actively suggesting, recommending, and assigning, the Council ratifies that which has already been informally agreed to by the calling body and the candidate, i.e., they formalize that which was informal.

In a sense, the role of the placement officers from the various synodical higher educational institutions possessing teacher education programs has changed. Certainly they are still consulted, but no longer to a significant degree by the Board of Assignments, or by the District president, or by the District school superintendent or education executive. Rather, the placement director is in consultation directly with officials of the calling body. Simultaneously, he or she attempts to keep District officials informed that they have had contact from one of its institutions, usually via e-mail to the District office confirming the sending of a credential file for the specific position.

The placement director's relationship to the candidate in this evolving process is also significantly different than it had been previously. Today, the placement director assumes, among others, the role of advocate, confidant, "counselor," and marketing agent.

Paradigm shifts, such as what procedures the Synod follows to place candidates into their first calls, tend to cause some whose perspective has become deeply rooted to balk rather strenuously. This may partially explain why controversy still manifests itself when the subject of the changing placement process for educational ministries is broached. Assessments equating the procedural changes presented thus far in this section with "an end around the Holy Spirit" reflect a negative critique.

Also, the procedural changes described above thus far have caused considerable concern for those involved with synodical placement of pastoral candidates. The thought of pastoral candidates being interviewed by officials of a calling congregation has in the past caused some agitation. Interestingly, recent practice suggests that the Synod's seminary placement officers and the Council of Presidents' pastoral placement subcommittee are allowing some congregations to interview pastoral candidates.

The change in placement procedures will in all likelihood continue. It needs to be noted, however, that synodical placement procedures fall under the rubric of adiaphora. If all involved in the calling of candidates for the church's various ministries continue to petition the Holy Spirit for guidance as they use their

---

[19] *Handbook of The Lutheran Church—Missouri Synod: 1998 Edition*, 24.

God-given rational powers, we are assured of the success of whatever frail procedures may evolve and be established in the future.

PROFESSIONAL SATISFACTION IN THE TEACHING MINISTRY

Once people become Lutheran teachers, are they generally satisfied with their service? While there is a significant need for comprehensive research within the Missouri Synod regarding this issue, in a relatively recent study Lutheran elementary school teachers in Michigan were asked, "All in all, how satisfied would you say you are with teaching as a career?" Of the 701 respondents, 94 percent said that they were either "very satisfied" or "somewhat satisfied."[20] Two important reasons for the Michigan Lutheran teachers' job satisfaction were their interaction with students and the spiritual dimension involved with Lutheran teaching, such as the opportunity to share their faith.[21]

Many of the Lutheran teachers in this sample, however, reported dissatisfaction with certain aspects of their ministry. "Salary and time were the two areas of most dissatisfaction. Forty-seven percent of teachers surveyed [were] not satisfied with the salary they received. In the area of time needed to complete the job, forty-eight percent of the teachers were dissatisfied."[22] Here, Lutheran teachers "feel a pull in opposite directions. They feel moral obligations to both families and their jobs. One teacher commented, 'It seems a shame that we say families are so important and yet our own families get short-changed.'"[23] Improvements in Lutheran teacher salaries and a better understanding by congregations of the pressures placed on teachers may reduce these aspects of dissatisfaction in the future.

STRESS, BURNOUT, AND ATTRITION

The teaching ministry has its difficult and stressful moments that could lead to "burnout" among some of those in service. Definitions of burnout generally characterize it as emotional and, in many cases, physical exhaustion. These reactions often stem from, among other factors, high expectations of those served and from ourselves, low pay, a sense of powerlessness, and unresolved conflicts.

Olsen points out that taking time away from the "church" world, exercise, having a support system, doing some things strictly for self, change of routine, and possessing realistic expectations and attitudes may be helpful stress relievers.

---

[20] William V. Hinz, "Job Satisfaction Among Lutheran Teachers," *Lutheran Education* 129 (January–February 1994), 123.

[21] Hinz, "Job Satisfaction Among Lutheran Teachers," 130.

[22] Hinz, "Job Satisfaction Among Lutheran Teachers," 124–125.

[23] Hinz, "Job Satisfaction Among Lutheran Teachers," 130.

Most importantly, she encourages time with God when one "can be passively open to God and He can come to us with His message."[24]

Today a greater number of people are leaving the Synod's pastoral and teaching service than are entering. In April and May 1999, Dr. Bruce Hartung, director of the Missouri Synod's Health Ministries with the Synod's Board for Human Care Ministries, asked those who read "Pressure Points," a column he writes for the *Reporter* (a monthly newspaper for the Synod's church leaders), to offer their opinions as to why people were leaving. More than 100 readers responded.

The following "voices" are those of Lutheran school teachers arranged by problem areas. These problems are not necessarily listed in terms of relative importance.

RESPECT

- Parents will no longer take the teacher's word over the child's word.

- Many parents want to assess blame. Often I am the target. I want to work together to focus on identifying the problems with a student and finding a solution.

- It's all related to the stress of working with young parents who were more concerned with protecting their children rather than facing consequences, and who couldn't say "no" to their children and didn't understand anyone's approach who could.

CONFLICT

- Endless, malicious gossip and a failure to implement Matthew 18 in dealings with teachers, students, families and other staff. ... It was this that, in the end, caused me to throw in the towel.

- As hard as it is to say this, the major personal issues that I and my friends in the teaching ministry have had are with pastors who don't see us as part of the team and hardly ever give a respectful word of encouragement.

- Official calls are not issued, contracts are "understood" to protect congregations from the process of getting rid of a "called" teacher who doesn't work out. The "call" has taken on the meaning of "called on contract," but the word "call" is sometimes used to placate the candidate and make him/her feel better.

SALARY

- Budgets are balanced and building projects are carried out on the backs of the low salaries of church workers.

---

[24] Linda Olsen, "Extra-Ministry Stress Relievers," *Lutheran Education* 122 (March–April 1987), 230–236.

- This should put the question to bed! Until congregations place a stronger emphasis on the ministry of the church by supporting it financially, church workers will continue to leave the profession to find some place that values their expertise.

- Many of my friends and my own family qualify for food stamps and free lunches because our wages were so low. Of course, I did not become a Lutheran teacher to earn money, but neither did I become a Lutheran teacher to subsidize the church.

- Plunder and false expectations are two of the root causes of our troubles. By "plunder," I mean the vast majority of our congregations who subsidize their general fund by impoverishing their teachers. Hundreds of congregations stalemate for about three months each year fighting over teachers' salaries.

- When I hear what our parochial school teachers are expected to live on, I am embarrassed to be part of this church body. Most of my friends who went to college with me and went into teaching are no longer serving. They simply found it necessary to take jobs outside the church in order to provide for their families.

PARENTHOOD

- I left the full-time ministry for motherhood. During my ministry, I came to the very strong conviction that the primary place of faith nurture is the home. Many of my female colleagues left for the same reason. Some think I am "wasting" my education and gifts, but my senior pastor wisely said that I have chosen a higher calling. I don't know if I will ever return to professional ministry.

- I made a choice between my vocation as a father and husband and my vocation as a teacher. I found I could not do both because of the low salary and the high demands of what seemed like a 24-hour-a-day job. I opted for being a father and a husband and found another teaching position outside of the LCMS system.

CULTURE

- Our society has diminished the stature and relevance of the church and those who serve there. So, our people come to church with a secular mindset. Once in leadership roles, they function from what they know best: a secular worldview and approach.

- Society is becoming increasingly at odds with the ministries of Lutheran schools and churches. We, as church workers, are finding ourselves further and further out of the range of society's norms. The church and its workers are coming under fire as this world in which we live moves itself further from God's will.25

Hartung points out that in these voices "can be heard pain, hope, anger, and honesty" and that "[t]here likely will be attempts to discount these voices. But," he cautions, "it is always in the voices of those pushed to the margins, of those distressed, of those who have walked through the valley that we can find the truths connected with an issue or concern."26

Hartung also points out that when church workers discuss why they have chosen to remain in, rather than leave, their positions, they "have pointed to their call to ministry—a call that is Spirit-inspired, and often experienced at very deep emotional and spiritual levels." He observes that the Synod's

> church workers often have a vision of themselves and others in Lutheran schools and congregations as working together for the greater mission of the proclamation and enactment of the Gospel. This desire ... is deeply felt and directly linked to the amount of support felt by workers. Conversely, its absence is linked to the amount of pressure felt.27

Hartung concludes that

> where people are broadly united in mission, there is a great deal of support for the worker; but where people have unresolved, festering or chronic con- flicts related to their mission, their personalities or prior events in the life of the worker or congregation, there is a sense of distress. It appears that ... the [failure to retain] church workers can be traced to the breakdown of the sense of being jointly committed to the mission of the local place, and the failure of structures (like the District and Synod) to be supportive.28

Overall, we have seen that Lutheran teachers are motivated by a call to ser- vice in God's kingdom. There is evidence that Lutheran teachers are satisfied with most aspects of their ministry. There appears to be some dissatisfaction, especially involving the resources of time and money, but also involving respect, conflict, parenting, and tensions of cultural dynamics. This dissatisfaction can lead to the problem of stress for the Lutheran teacher who has not yet learned to cope with it and also contributes to attrition from service.

---

[25] Bruce Hartung, "The LCMS Is Losing Good Workers. The Question Is Why?" *Reporter* (June 1999), 8.

[26] Hartung, "The LCMS Is Losing Good Workers," 8.

[27] Hartung, "The LCMS Is Losing Good Workers," 8.

[28] Hartung, "The LCMS Is Losing Good Workers," 8.

PERSONAL AND PROFESSIONAL DEVELOPMENT

While certainly not a panacea, Lutheran school teachers who take responsibility for their personal and professional growth will likely find effective assistance in counteracting some dissatisfaction with their ministry. It goes without saying that maintaining an active worship and prayer life is the foundation of one's personal growth. Building on that footing are the many inservice opportunities available to the Lutheran school teacher.

The Lutheran educator is both a minister and a professional. As a professional, he or she will continually strive to improve himself or herself. This requires a lifetime commitment.

Various avenues for professional development are open to the Lutheran teacher. For example, many states now require teachers to participate in professional development programs in order to maintain their state teaching licenses. For those new to the teaching ministry, pursuit of a master's degree via graduate study is an excellent means by which to address this requirement. Of course, participation in specialized workshops or inservice training is also usually available for compliance purposes. While both options may be viewed simply as an approach to address state mandates, Lutheran school teachers understand that graduate work and involvement in workshops and inservice training are ways to improve their professional skills, thereby enhancing their ministry to God's people.

Membership in the Lutheran Education Association is another opportunity for personal and professional development. This 4,500-plus member organization was founded in 1942 to promote Christian education in the home, school, and parish. The association provides an option to join one of its special interest departments supporting the Lutheran early childhood teacher, elementary teacher, school administrator, or director of Christian education. The primary mission of the Lutheran Education Association today is to link, equip, and affirm educators in Lutheran ministries. Anyone who attends one of the organization's triennial national convocations certainly experiences the exhilaration of that linkage, equipping, and affirmation.

In addition to the Lutheran Education Association, Lutheran teachers may also benefit from membership in specialized professional organizations for teachers such as the following:

- American Alliance for Health, Physical Education, Recreation and Dance
- International Reading Association
- Music Teachers National Association
- National Art Education Association
- National Association for the Education of the Young Child
- National Council for the Social Studies

- National Council of Teachers of English
- National Council of Teachers of Mathematics
- National Science Teachers Association

The above list, while not exhaustive, represents organizations that should contribute to the professional growth of many Lutheran early childhood, elementary, and secondary teachers.

In addition, synodical District teachers conferences and local faculty meetings offer additional opportunities for the Lutheran teacher to grow both personally and professionally. Lutheran teachers conferences, which have been held since 1854, offer, among other things, a wide choice of sectionals that address a variety of topics designed to equip the teacher for improvement in various spheres of ministry. Faculty meetings, especially those that go beyond routine business and take up areas of the Lutheran school program for special study, also can contribute to the development of the Lutheran teacher.

The aforementioned examples of opportunities recognize that personal and professional growth do not terminate upon receipt of a college diploma. Moreover, and most importantly, these activities provide arenas in which Lutheran teachers can encourage one another. All can understand the relationship between encouragement and satisfaction.

Summing Up

There appears to be currently and for the immediate future a serious shortage of teachers for Lutheran schools, especially in such areas as computer-science education, early childhood and elementary education, mathematics, music, and science. Preservice Lutheran teacher education programs are designed to prepare successful teaching ministers who are liberally educated, theologically well-grounded, and professionally competent. Lutheran teachers are affected by the varying state-by-state requirements for certification and are also subject to a synodical certification process leading to their first call into the teaching ministry. The initial placement process has changed over decades with both candidate and calling body having much more involvement. This change has not occurred without controversy. While evidence suggests that many Lutheran teachers are satisfied with most aspects of their ministry, there is also evidence suggesting that Lutheran teachers are dissatisfied with salaries, the lack of time they have for effective performance of their tasks, a perceived lack of respect, the ongoing conflicts involved with those whom they serve and serve with, their ability to parent their own children, and the impact of cultural change upon the church. Perhaps because of this dissatisfaction, more individuals continue to leave rather than enter Lutheran school teaching. It is suggested that personal and professional growth initiatives may serve to alleviate some of this dissatisfaction through opportunities these activities offer for mutual encouragement.

DISCUSSION TOPICS AND SUGGESTED PROJECTS

1. What steps can be taken to improve the salaries of Lutheran teachers? Which are most likely to be successful? What will determine whether they are successful?

2. Collect and analyze information on teacher salary schedules in several near-by Lutheran schools. Compare your data with information other members of your class acquire from additional Lutheran schools. What patterns do you see?

3. Survey current Lutheran teachers regarding their perceptions of the synodical teacher education program that prepared them for service in Lutheran schools. Ask for recommendations for improving preservice Lutheran teacher education.

4. Invite the individual from your college or university faculty or staff who is responsible for synodical teacher placement. Ask him or her to address Lutheran teacher supply and demand and state certification and to explain how synodical certification is conducted at your institution.

5. Interview a Lutheran elementary school teacher and a Lutheran high school teacher about their level of satisfaction with their ministry and their reasons for being satisfied or dissatisfied. Compare your findings with those of other students in your class.

6. Imagine that you have been in the teaching ministry for five years. Generate a list of reasons why your service is satisfying and a list of reasons why it may not be.

7. Interview a Lutheran teacher who has left the ministry for another career. Identify his or her reasons for leaving and current feelings about the choice.

RESOURCES, INFLUENCES, AND SUGGESTED FURTHER READING

"Commissioned Ministers of Religion: 1998–99 Placement Statistics." St. Louis: Board for Higher Education, The Lutheran Church—Missouri Synod, 1999.

Einspahr, Glenn C. "State Certification Trends." *Lutheran Education* 119 (November–December 1983): 104–113.

Handbook of The Lutheran Church—Missouri Synod: 1998 Edition. St. Louis: The Lutheran Church—Missouri Synod, 1998.

Heinitz, Kenneth. "The Handling of a Call: A Response." *Lutheran Education* 124 (January–February 1989): 299–305.

Hinz, William V. "Job Satisfaction Among Lutheran Teachers." *Lutheran Education* 129 (January–February 1994): 123–133.

Holtzen, Lee Roy, and Roy C. Krause. "Teacher Placement in the LC-MS." Pages 17–40 in *The Role of the Lutheran Teacher*. 8th ed. Seward, Nebr.: Graphic Printing Company, 1997.

Lehmann, William, Jr. "New Directions in Teacher Placement." *Lutheran Education* 113 (September–October 1977): 32–35.

Moser, Carl, ed. *The Call of the Lutheran Teacher*. St. Louis: School Ministry Department, The Lutheran Church—Missouri Synod, n.d.

Mueller, Arnold C. "The Call of the Christian Teacher." Pages 124–147 in *The Ministry of the Lutheran Teacher: A Study to Determine the Position of the Lutheran Parish School Teacher within the Public Ministry of the Church*. St. Louis: Concordia Publishing House, 1964.

Olsen, Linda. "Extra-Ministry Stress Relievers." *Lutheran Education* 122 (March–April 1987): 230–236.

Procedures for Calling Commissioned Ministers in The Lutheran Church—Missouri Synod. St. Louis: The Board for Higher Education and Congregational Services, The Lutheran Church—Missouri Synod, 1999.

Rietschel, William C. "The Synodical Placement Process: Past and Present." *Lutheran Education* 128 (March–April 1993): 204–211.

Stelmachowicz, Michael J. "Myths and Trends: Placement of Teachers." *Lutheran Education* 101 (May 1966): 409–413.

Stueber, Ross E., ed. "1998–99 Statistical Report Summary, Schools and Early Childhood Centers of The Lutheran Church—Missouri Synod." St. Louis: Department of School Ministry, The Lutheran Church—Missouri Synod, 1999.

Tryneski, John, ed. *Requirements for Certification*. 64th ed. Chicago: University of Chicago Press, 1999–2000.

Zillman, O. John. "Lutheran Teacher Supply and Demand." Unpublished survey, Office of Educational and Synodical Placement, River Forest, Ill., August 1999.

7

GOVERNANCE AND FINANCING
OF LUTHERAN SCHOOLS

Prospective Lutheran teachers eventually hope to secure and accept a teaching position in a Lutheran school. After acceptance, Lutheran teachers will be affected by numerous policies emanating from a variety of structures.

Lutheran educators need to know not only who the "players" are but also how they work together to shape and implement Lutheran school policy. This chapter and the next will explore the polity as well as the economic and legal foundations of Lutheran schools.

GOVERNING AND ADMINISTERING
LUTHERAN SCHOOLS

To serve students effectively and foster congregational or high school association objectives, the Lutheran school's governance and administration must proceed according to certain principles. For example, the policy-making and policy-executing agents must be clearly defined. Where responsibility is delegated, sufficient authority must also be delegated. It is to these concerns and others that we now turn our attention.[1]

CONGREGATIONAL POLITY: VOTERS' ASSEMBLY

The Lutheran congregation, an assembly of persons coming together for religious worship or teaching, is the fundamental structural component of The Lutheran Church—Missouri Synod. Without it, there is no need for any other structural layers.

---

[1] This section is substantially an amalgam of excerpts adapted from the following sources: Glenn Bracht, *Planning for Lutheran Elementary Schools: Board of Education Handbook* (St. Louis: Board of Parish Education, The Lutheran Church—Missouri Synod, 1978); Bill Cochran, *Lutheran School Administrator's Handbook: Leadership* (St. Louis: School Services Department, The Lutheran Church—Missouri Synod, 1995); Theodore P. Gerken, "The Lutheran Elementary School and the Congregation," in *Lutheran Elementary Schools in Action* (ed. Victor C. Krause; St. Louis: Concordia Publishing House, 1963); Edward J. Keuer, "The School and The Lutheran Church—Missouri Synod," in *Lutheran Elementary Schools in Action* (ed. Victor C. Krause; St. Louis: Concordia Publishing House, 1963); and Martin F. Wessler, *Lutheran Schools 21st Century: Governance and Management* (St. Louis: Board for Parish Services, The Lutheran Church—Missouri Synod, 1993).

Every Lutheran congregation operates some type of program for education. Because they vary in size and are impacted by local conditions and leadership, congregations do their work each in their own unique manner. However, all congregations will have some type of organizational structure relating to educational programming specified by their constitution and bylaws. Some are complex; others quite basic. Figure 7.1 is an example of the latter.

FIGURE 7.1:
Congregational Organizational Structure for Education

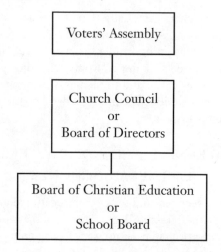

The congregation is also a legal corporation and as such owns and operates its elementary school. Traditionally, school governance was a responsibility of the voters' assembly. Over the years this has changed, and the current practice is more typically for the voters' assembly to delegate immediate control of the elementary school to either a board of Christian education or to a school board. At the same time, however, the voters' assembly reserves to itself the right to decide major issues in policy, administration, or program. These arrangements would be reflected in the congregation's constitution.

CONGREGATIONAL POLITY:
CHURCH COUNCIL OR BOARD OF DIRECTORS

To expedite their constitutional directives, many congregations will organize their board of Christian education or school board so that it relates to the congregation through the church council or a board of directors (Figure 7.1). The church council or board of directors typically comprises the chairs of all other congregational boards, e.g., elders, finance, trustees, etc., in addition to a president, vice-president, secretary, and treasurer. The church council or board of directors also supervises the work of these boards and, at its regular monthly meetings, hears reports from them.

CONGREGATIONAL POLITY:
BOARD OF CHRISTIAN EDUCATION OR SCHOOL BOARD

Some Lutheran congregations assign all responsibilities for Christian education and all Christian education agencies to one board generally called the board of Christian education. Other congregations assign school management to a separate board, usually known as a school board, to devote its attention and efforts only to the school.

The board of Christian education is usually responsible for all Christian education activities in the congregation, including the Lutheran school, Sunday school, adult education, vacation Bible school, confirmation classes, and other educational agencies and activities. The board for efficiency purposes may organize itself into committees, e.g., school, Sunday school and vacation Bible school, adult education, and youth. Here, the school committee would perform the functions of a school board, but the formal approval of policies and other major decisions remain the responsibility of the total board of Christian education. A separate school board normally is responsible only for the operation of the congregation's school. For consistency and clarity purposes, the subsequent treatment will use the nomenclature school board.

The school board is the duly elected (or appointed) agent of the congregation. Its function is governance of the Lutheran school. As such, the board guides, steers, directs, and supervises the overall operation of the school. The board governs on behalf of the congregation to which it is accountable.

Regardless of size or level, i.e., early childhood, elementary, or secondary, there are three essential functions of the board in the operation of a Lutheran school. They are policy-making, supervision, and management.

The primary function of the school board is to establish *policy*, whereby it assures that all aspects of the school's operation are well managed. Through its policies the board can direct and manage all components of school operation including supervision of the principal and staff, finances and facilities, and curriculum and student life. Policies are clear statements expressing the views and directives of the board for managing the school and providing guidelines for the ongoing administration of the school.

The board's *supervisory* function is reflected in its management of most aspects of the school program through its policies and through the supervision of the principal and staff as they carry out the board's policy. In some instances, the board may become involved in direct supervision of financial-planning and facilities-planning activities.

As the previous paragraph implies, *management* of the school operation is exercised as the board establishes policy and supervises the principal and staff. A board is also managing the school's operation when it establishes a policy regarding tuition and fees, calling and engaging staff members, setting school calendars, and salary schedules.

Because Lutheran schools frequently are an integral part of the congregation's ministry and administration, several areas of management and administration need to be considered further. These include management of finances, facilities, and building programs.

The school board is responsible for seeing to it that budgets and financial projections are prepared annually and that adequate funding is available to accomplish the ultimate ends of the Lutheran school. Because of variations in the structure of congregations, the final responsibilities for these activities may rest with the school board, the church finance committee, or the church council or board of directors. In some instances, the school budget may be the full responsibility of congregational financial officers.

In the area of facility management and building programs, congregational structures differ in the assignment of responsibility. The school board may have a major responsibility for school facilities, or this may be the responsibility of a board of trustees or other similar committees. In any case, theoretically, the board should take an active role to insure that facilities are adequate to achieve the objectives of the school, which includes the equipping, maintaining, and expanding of school facilities.

The number of members on a board may vary relative to the size of the school, size of the congregation, and the responsibilities assigned to the board. As a rule, board membership ranges between five and seven members. Both pastor and school administrator serve as *ex officio* (nonvoting) members of the board.

Congregational policies specify the length of term for board members. A term of two or three years is typical and insures continuity in management of the school. Also to insure continuity, terms do not expire simultaneously.

School boards can be effectively organized in a variety of ways. Boards may have both standing and *ad hoc* (concerned with a particular end or purpose) committees. Committees are often used for budget planning, facility analysis, program evaluation, or other similar assignments. However, all reports and decisions are reserved for the board as a whole.

Minutes are kept of every board meeting along with reports and other essential materials. Usually a complete set of the board's minutes and other board records are maintained in the school. Some states require this.

CONGREGATIONAL POLITY:
THE ROLE OF THE PASTOR IN LUTHERAN SCHOOL GOVERNANCE

The pastor has been called to be the spiritual leader of the congregation. As such he needs to be concerned with, and also philosophically supportive of, the congregation's program of Christian education. He must have an overview of all the congregation's educational activities, encouraging wherever possible the coordination of these activities. The pastor's role in the administration and supervision is advisory and stems from his concern for the overall welfare of the congregation. The importance of the pastor in policy making is to assure that the Lutheran school will remain distinctively Christian.

CONGREGATIONAL POLITY:
THE PRINCIPAL AND THE LUTHERAN SCHOOL

The principal holds a key role in successful management of the Lutheran school. In a sense, management is the function of the school administrator (principal or director) as he or she carries out the responsibility for administering on a day-to-day basis all essential functions in the operation of the school in accord with the policies set by the board. Simply, the board sets policy and the principal carries it out. The administrator is the person in charge on behalf of the board, the leader of the school's ministry.

In addition to serving as manager of the Lutheran school, the principal serves as the director of the school's educational program and ministry as well as the leader for school climate. These responsibilities are fulfilled in accord with the school's mission and in harmony with established policies. The administrator develops and carries out plans and programs to achieve the responsibilities assigned. He or she consults and confers with the board in developing plans and carrying out responsibilities. In addition, because the administrator is accountable to the board, he or she reports regularly to the board regarding the progress and effectiveness of these plans and programs.

The functional responsibilities of the Lutheran school administrator break down in the following manner:

1. School Manager
   - Public Relations and Communications
   - Office Management
   - Student Recruitment and Admissions
   - Financial Planning and Accounting
   - Executive Administrator

2. Director of School Educational Programs and Ministry
   - School Curriculum Development
   - Supervision of Teachers and Instruction

3. Leader for School Climate
   - Leadership for Spiritual Life
   - Student Life
   - Building and Grounds
   - Care for Workers
   - Discipline

Undergirding all of these functions is the mission of the Lutheran school administrator (and staff for that matter) to deliberately witness and model Christ's love for the Lutheran school family.

CONSOLIDATION: THE LUTHERAN SCHOOL ASSOCIATION

Sometimes called interparish or central schools, consolidated schools are supported by more than one congregation. Consolidated schools are usually found in one of two situations (or in combination):

- Two or more small neighboring congregations cannot support individual schools, but are strong enough to maintain a school together.

- A large congregation has a school and is well able to maintain it, but to provide school advantages also for children of the smaller congregations, it enters into an association arrangement.

Governance of the consolidated school calls for a board that is constituted of representatives from each congregation participating in the association. Its responsibilities would be similar to an individual congregation's school board.

THE LUTHERAN HIGH SCHOOL

Usually, a Lutheran high school is supported by an association of congregations. If so, the governance model would be akin to that of the consolidated Lutheran elementary school. A few Lutheran high schools are conducted by a single Missouri Synod parish, in which case their governance would come under the congregation school board.

THE ROLE OF THE SYNOD AND DISTRICT

Authority for an existing relationship between the school and the Synod is based on the Synod's constitution and bylaws as found in the *Handbook: The Lutheran Church—Missouri Synod.*[2] The Synod and its member congregations are bound to the principles and regulations agreed on in the *Handbook*. References to schools (excepting higher education) in the constitution are quite general, but are more detailed in the bylaws. The bylaws also delegate certain responsibilities to various departments of the Synod.

The more general references governing the relationship of the Synod to Lutheran schools are contained in the objectives of the Synod as found in Article III of the constitution. These charge the Synod with recruiting and training teachers, aiding congregations in establishing Lutheran elementary and secondary schools and providing them with resources, and providing for the super-

---

[2] *Handbook of The Lutheran Church—Missouri Synod: 1998 Edition* (St. Louis: The Lutheran Church—Missouri Synod, 1998).

vision, protection, and welfare of teachers.[3] The Synod has historically taken the position that the most effective agencies available to the church for equipping God's people for ministry are Lutheran elementary and secondary schools.

There are other constitutional references concerning schools. Articles V and VI give authority for called teachers to hold advisory membership in the Synod.[4] Article XII encourages District presidents to "exercise supervision over the doctrine, life, and administration of office of the ordained and commissioned ministers [includes teachers] of their District and acquaint themselves with the religious conditions of the congregations of their District."[5] Article XII also requires District presidents to "[p]erform, either in person or by proxy … the installation of the candidates for the office of schoolteacher and of all … teachers called by congregations in their District."[6] Article XIII gives procedures governing expulsion of a member from the Synod.[7] This can pertain to teachers as well as congregations.

In order to carry out its constitutional responsibilities toward Lutheran schools, the Synod acts officially in convention, supervises through its office of the president and its board of directors, and assigns policy-making and executive powers to its various boards, commissions, departments, and committees. The Synod's Department of School Ministry has responsibility for Lutheran elementary and secondary schools in this regard, while early childhood education is the responsibility of the Department of Child Ministry.

Synod is also organized into smaller units called Districts. The 35 Districts in the United States tend to follow state boundaries with the exception of the English District and the Slovak Evangelical Lutheran Church. Districts are also broken down into smaller administrative units called circuits.

While the relationship between the school and the Synod is primarily voluntary and somewhat remote, the relationship of the Lutheran school to the District, while also primarily voluntary, is more specific and direct. Generally, the Synod's service to Lutheran schools is more promotional and supportive, whereas that of the District's service is more advisory.

Lutheran schools would have a significantly more difficult task without the services of the Synod and the District. Among these many services are supplying synodically trained teachers, instructional materials (especially for teaching religion), professional publications, financial subsidy for mission schools, promotional programs and materials, professional advice and counseling, legal assistance, in-service educational opportunities, and the like.

---

[3] *Handbook of The Lutheran Church—Missouri Synod: 1998 Edition*, 9–10.

[4] *Handbook of The Lutheran Church—Missouri Synod: 1998 Edition*, 10–11.

[5] *Handbook of The Lutheran Church—Missouri Synod: 1998 Edition*, 14.

[6] *Handbook of The Lutheran Church—Missouri Synod: 1998 Edition*, 15.

[7] *Handbook of The Lutheran Church—Missouri Synod: 1998 Edition*, 16.

Since the primary contact of a Lutheran school teacher is with the District education executive, it is important for those entering the teaching ministry to understand the District executive's role. "[T]he ... education executive or someone with similar responsibilities ... assists the president [of the District] in ministry among the educators in the District in the role of 'personnel' manager." In addition, according to Keith Loomans, "The exec is involved in all aspects of school ministry and works with all involved in the process of developing and maintaining excellence in school ministry."[8] Among the roles played by the District education executive are the following:

1. *encourager* of all involved in educational ministries;

2. *challenger* of teachers to function at their highest level of competence and effectiveness;

3. *facilitator* of educator growth and development through guiding the development of conference programs and other in-service activity;

4. *equipper/trainer* via leading various workshops, seminars, and conference sectionals;

5. *resourcers/brokers* as, for example, in developing call lists for congregations and counseling congregations planning to call graduates;

6. *definer/clarifier* of call procedures and terminology as well as of national, state, and local educational laws and practice;

7. *evaluator* of the District's classroom teachers and school administrators;

8. *visionary* in the process of determining the scope and future mission of the school as it is involved in functioning as a strong resource of the congregation; and lastly,

9. *shepherd* praying for all who labor in the kingdom, supporting the spiritual growth of educators, grieving when they grieve, celebrating when they celebrate.[9]

Finally, and also within the context of governance, Figure 7.2 attempts to portray the relationship of the Lutheran school to the state as well as to the Synod and to its parent congregation. Consequently, it serves as a good summary of this segment of the chapter. The lines of direct authority from the state agencies indicate that local Lutheran school governance recognizes the authority of the state with respect to such matters as attendance, building codes, safety regulations, and certain curricular requirements. The lines of informational and

---

[8] Keith Loomans, "The District Exec, A Partner in Ministry, A Friend in Need," *Lutheran Education* 128 (March–April 1993), 194.

[9] Loomans, "The District Exec, A Partner in Ministry, A Friend in Need," 194–196.

advisory contact from the synodical agencies to the local board reflect the counseling relationship that exists between the District and the local board.

More information regarding governmental and legal aspects of Lutheran education will be presented in the next chapter. However, we now turn our attention to the financing of Lutheran education.

FINANCING LUTHERAN SCHOOLS

When members of Lutheran congregations appreciate the value of the Lutheran school, they appear to be willing to support it. When parents are persuaded of the unique contributions of a Lutheran school, they appear willing to provide support to insure its continued operation. When congregation members are convinced that the school is serving the ends of Lutheran education for families, it appears that financial support is generally available from the congregational budget.[10]

FIGURE 7.2

Lutheran Elementary School Organization

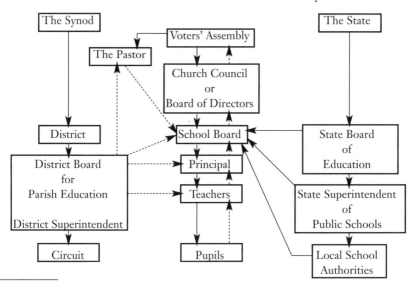

———— Line of direct authority

············ Line of informational and advisory contact

---

[10] This section is substantially an amalgam of excerpts adapted from the following sources: Lee Roy Holtzen and Roy C. Krause, "Finances in the Life of the Lutheran School and Teacher," in *The Role of the Lutheran Teacher* (8th ed.; Seward, Nebr.: Graphic Printing Company, 1997); Neal Meitler and Martin F. Wessler, *Planning for Lutheran Elementary Schools: Funding Lutheran Elementary Schools* (St. Louis: Board of Parish Education, The Lutheran Church—Missouri Synod, 1978); Robert Rogalski, *Lutheran School Administrator's Handbook: Funding* (St. Louis: School Services Department, The Lutheran Church—Missouri Synod, 1995); and Martin F. Wessler, *Lutheran Schools 21st Century: Funding Lutheran Schools* (St. Louis: Board for Parish Services, The Lutheran Church—Missouri Synod, 1993).

Lutheran schools cost money. Careful planning is needed to justify expenditures and insure that the Lutheran school is meeting the objectives of the congregation for ministry to children and their parents. Sound Lutheran education and high-quality instructional programs can justify the financial outlays for a school.

A Brief History of Lutheran School Funding

For many years Lutheran schools in this country were financed principally through the local congregation. The parish assumed responsibility for the education of its young people and, outside of their regular church contributions, parents assumed little of the cost. All member children attended the Lutheran school. In fact, not to attend was almost regarded as being heretical. Often non-member children, considered mission prospects, also attended tuition free. For many parishes a Lutheran school was considered an obligation.

As costs escalated, congregations found it more and more difficult to fulfill their obligation to operate a school without a charge to parents. This resulted in classifying children who attended the Lutheran school into four categories:

1. Children whose parents were members of the congregation who paid no tuition since it was assumed that their parents were contributing through the general treasury.

2. Children who, with their parents, had no church home and were considered mission prospects, thus paying no tuition.

3. Children whose parents belonged to other Lutheran congregations.

4. Children whose parents were members of non-Lutheran churches.

Those who were in the last two categories either were charged tuition or were asked to make a donation to help defray school expenses.

Current funding sources for Lutheran schools are congregational income, tuition and fees, development income, fund-raising, endowments, and special projects funded through the government or other agencies. During 1998–1999, 52 percent of Lutheran elementary school funding was received from tuition and fees, 42 percent from the congregation budget, and 6 percent was received from other sources.[11]

Congregational Income

As already indicated, for many years most Lutheran schools in this country were financed principally through the congregation's budget. And this is still the primary means of financial support for elementary schools. However, as the cost of Lutheran schools has increased due to lower pupil-teacher ratios and more

---

[11] Ross E. Stueber, ed., "1998–99 Statistical Report Summary, Schools and Early Childhood Centers of The Lutheran Church—Missouri Synod" (St. Louis: Department of School Ministry, The Lutheran Church—Missouri Synod, 1999), 6.

costly instructional programs and techniques, many congregations are now unable to finance the total operation. Consequently, there are any number of Lutheran schools that are funded almost entirely by tuition and fees.

The many congregations that have historically relied totally on congregational support built their case on the premise that Christian education is a basic responsibility of the church and, therefore, the cost of it should be shared by all members in the congregation. Congregation members who used other services of the congregation were not asked to pay a pro-rata share of the cost for these services. Therefore, neither should some members have been asked to pay a pro-rata share of the cost for educating their children.

Currently, commitment from the congregation can range from no support to a commitment of the total school budget. Neither extreme is chosen very often by Lutheran congregations. Even congregations that are committed to school support through the church budget choose to have some school costs financed by fees and other outside sources of income.

Some Districts provide a subsidy to finance Lutheran schools in cases of mission congregations, central-city congregations, and parishes in transitional situations. In these cases, when a congregation seeks to maintain a school, a subsidy enables the congregation to fulfill its role in support of the school.

TUITION AND FEES

The tuition movement began in the early 1940s as new Lutheran schools were started premised on a tuition funding approach. Many of these newly opened schools charged tuition to everyone who had children enrolled, although the amount was differentiated between members and nonmembers. The funding philosophy was changing and the basic premise was now that parents, not the congregation, bore financial responsibility for Christian education—at least as it related to the Lutheran school.

The majority of Lutheran schools across the country now charge tuition to member and nonmember families. More and more schools are accepting the premise that parents should share in the direct responsibility of providing a Christian education for their children. Many congregations that charge tuition and fees do so as a matter of economic necessity.

If a congregation has determined that tuition will be charged for members and/or nonmembers, the tuition rate is established fairly based on the actual cost of educating a child. Using cost-per-pupil as the criterion helps avoid making arbitrary decisions.

Fees for bus service, lunches, books, materials, registration, and other items are usually charged in addition to tuition. Establishing these fees is based on a reasonably close estimate of their actual cost as well.

A variety of tuition structures are available to Lutheran schools, which allow rates to vary depending on the number of children in the family, the economic level of the family, and the type of program. Among the options available are

1. A fixed tuition charge for every child.

2. Reduced tuition for the second and third child in the family. Sometimes the third or fourth child in the family is allowed to attend at no cost.

3. Kindergarten students attending half days are often charged one-half of the regular tuition rate.

4. Rates for early childhood programs are often based on the cost-per-pupil and may be calculated on a different basis than the elementary school tuition.

5. Tuition rates may be based on a sliding scale that is related to family income. Low-income families are required to pay lesser amounts. This method necessitates record keeping and submission of personal-income figures by parents.

6. "Negotiated tuition" is another variation of option number 5. In this case, parents and the administrator confer to determine what rate is fair to the school and within the reach of the parents. Some parents may pay very little, while others pay the full cost-per-pupil.

7. Members are often charged a lower tuition rate than nonmembers because members are contributing toward the total work of the parish through their regular church contributions.

Tuition payments for elementary education cannot be used by parents as tax deductions. In cases where parents are required to make minimum contributions to the parish in lieu of tuition payments, the Internal Revenue Service has ruled that these are the same as tuition and, therefore, not deductible. Congregations should not publish fixed minimums.

As the cost of education continues to increase, families are being asked to pay higher tuition and fees for their children to attend a Lutheran school. While some schools have charged tuition to all students for a number of years, the trends indicate that most schools will charge tuition or an education fee of a significant amount to their own members in the future. For those who already charge tuition to members, the trends also indicate that this fee is increasing rapidly. In recognition of this rapid increase and the fact that not all families can equally afford tuition payments, a student aid fund is provided by many Lutheran schools to meet the needs of parents who cannot make full tuition payments.

DEVELOPMENT INCOME

Development income, i.e., special gifts solicited from a variety of sources, is an increasingly significant source for funding Lutheran schools. There are parents, other individuals, and organizations who may wish to donate funds to the school. Gifts of cash to the school can be solicited from a variety of sources and for a wide range of purposes. Some of the more common include local business and industries, foundations, gifts from individuals, memorial programs, and estates and bequests. Some donors prefer non-cash gifts and are able in this way to insure that the Lutheran school receives a particular item (e.g., classroom or office equipment), supplies, or service (e.g., painting, repair).

FUND-RAISING

Lutheran school fund-raising projects are generally sponsored by parent organizations, auxiliaries, or student groups. Most fund-raising projects involve solicitation activities and the sale of items or services. Perhaps the most common items sold by these groups are pizza, candy, fruit, or other consumable items.

While many Lutheran schools encourage some form of fund raising, they restrict it in a manner that is consistent with their educational program objectives. Income from fund-raising projects usually accounts for a rather small part of the Lutheran school's total financial program.

ENDOWMENTS

An endowment fund is a special reserve set aside to take care of emergencies and/or provide for the continuation of certain projects. It's like a personal savings or pension plan designed to build a principal sum large enough so that, some day, you can live off the interest earned. For a Lutheran school, the endowment can help the school's programs to continue even in bad economic times, or it can assure the success of a future project.

Increasingly, Lutheran schools are establishing endowments. In addition, The Lutheran Church—Missouri Synod has established the National Lutheran Elementary School Endowment. This fund provides a variety of assistance: grants for tuition aid for students, in-service activities and resources, teaching and learning equipment and materials, and special programs for special student needs.

GOVERNMENT-FUNDED PROGRAMS

Certain states and the federal government provide funding for services and programs on behalf of children attending Lutheran schools. These services and programs include such areas as transportation, textbooks, food services, specialized help for the disadvantaged, and others. "School Choice" programs are now operating in Wisconsin, Ohio, and Florida, to provide state assistance to low income families. Initial state court decisions have declared such programs to be a legitimate use of state-controlled money. However, there are also conflicting rulings between some state and federal courts regarding school choice plans, which may cause the United States Supreme Court to address the issue in the future. Normally government-funded programs do not interfere with the distinctive purpose of Lutheran schools. Nevertheless, Lutheran schools will need to scrutinize these programs for that possibility and not be blinded by need given current funding pressures.

Government-funded programs usually require application, record-keeping, supervision, and accountability. By participating in programs provided by the state and federal government, schools are agents in helping carry out those services and programs that the state deems important for all children of the state.

The Council for American Private Education (CAPE) is an effective monitor of federal aid programs and communicator of private school concerns to the United States Department of Education, the Congress, and related offices. Nearly all of the national Lutheran school systems are members of CAPE.

FUNDING THE LUTHERAN HIGH SCHOOL

Lutheran high schools typically are funded primarily by tuition, with some assistance from congregations and development sources. In 1998-1999, for example, 73 percent of Lutheran high school funding came from tuition and fees, only 8 percent from congregational budgets, and 18 percent from other sources.[12] If the Lutheran high school is incorporated as an association, the member congregations contribute to the per-pupil cost of education with tuition making up the remaining balance. Students from outside the association typically are responsible for the entire cost of tuition.

As costs increase faster than income, there will be increased pressure on Lutheran school finances and on the ability of sponsoring bodies, i.e., congregations and associations, to fund them. It seems inevitable that tuition, including member tuition, will be the primary source of Lutheran school funding.

SUMMING UP

Lutheran schools are governed by duly elected or appointed officers and committees. The school board has a variety of duties and responsibilities, as does the Lutheran school administrator. The nature of these responsibilities will vary with local conditions.

The relationship between the Lutheran school and the Synod and District is essentially voluntary and advisory. The congregation is an autonomous unit with generally complete administrative and supervisory power over its program.

Basic sources for funding Lutheran schools are the congregation, tuition and fees, development income, fund-raising, and some state and federal income. It appears, however, that Lutheran schools will increasingly become tuition driven.

---

[12] Stueber, "1998–99 Statistical Report Summary," 6.

DISCUSSION TOPICS AND SUGGESTED PROJECTS

1. Attend a local Lutheran school board meeting. Note who is present. Examine the meeting agenda. Then answer the following questions: (a) What topics and issues were discussed? (b) What views were expressed? (c) Were there differing or alternative views? How did the school board respond to these different viewpoints? (d) What decisions were made by the school board, and how were they reached? (e) What did you learn about Lutheran school governance from your attendance at the meeting?

2. How, as a Lutheran school teacher, can you influence educational change in a Lutheran school?

3. Invite a local Lutheran school administrator to speak to your class on the budget process.

4. Interview several members of a local Lutheran school board on school finance issues and problems. Report to the class on the trends that you discerned in your interviews.

5. Survey private-sector corporations in your locality to determine if they have programs such as the "matching gift" concept designed to support Lutheran schools.

RESOURCES, INFLUENCES, AND SUGGESTED FURTHER READING

Bracht, Glenn. *Planning for Lutheran Elementary Schools: Board of Education Handbook*. St Louis: Board of Parish Education, The Lutheran Church—Missouri Synod, 1978.

Cochran, Bill. *Lutheran School Administrator's Handbook: Leadership*. St. Louis: School Services Department, The Lutheran Church—Missouri Synod, 1995.

Engebrecht, Richard H. "Financing the Lutheran Elementary School." Pages 340–373 in *Lutheran Elementary Schools in Action*. Edited by Victor C. Krause. St. Louis: Concordia Publishing House, 1963.

Gerken, Theodore P. "The Lutheran Elementary School and the Congregation." Pages 84–111 in *Lutheran Elementary Schools in Action*. Edited by Victor C. Krause. St. Louis: Concordia Publishing House, 1963.

Handbook of The Lutheran Church—Missouri Synod: 1998 Edition. St. Louis: The Lutheran Church—Missouri Synod, 1998.

Holtzen, Lee Roy, and Roy C. Krause. "Finances in the Life of the Lutheran School and Teacher" in *The Role of the Lutheran Teacher*. 8th ed. Seward, Nebr.: Graphic Printing Company, 1997.

Keuer, Edward J. "The School and The Lutheran Church—Missouri Synod." Pages 112–139 in *Lutheran Elementary Schools in Action*. Edited by Victor C. Krause. St. Louis: Concordia Publishing House, 1963.

Loomans, Keith. "The District Exec, A Partner in Ministry, A Friend in Need." *Lutheran Education* 128 (March–April 1993): 191–196.

Meitler, Neal, and Martin Wessler. *Planning for Lutheran Elementary Schools: Funding Lutheran Elementary Schools*. St. Louis: Board of Parish Education, The Lutheran Church—Missouri Synod, 1978.

Rogalski, Robert. *Lutheran School Administrator's Handbook: Funding*. St. Louis: School Services Department, The Lutheran Church—Missouri Synod, 1995.

Stueber, Ross E., ed. "1998–99 Statistical Report Summary, Schools and Early Childhood Centers of The Lutheran Church—Missouri Synod." St. Louis: Department of School Ministry, The Lutheran Church—Missouri Synod, 1999.

Wessler, Martin F. *Lutheran Schools 21st Century: Funding Lutheran Schools*. St. Louis: Board for Parish Services, The Lutheran Church—Missouri Synod, 1993.

_____. *Lutheran Schools 21st Century: Governance and Management*. St. Louis: Board for Parish Services, The Lutheran Church—Missouri Synod, 1993.

8

LEGAL ASPECTS OF
LUTHERAN SCHOOLS

The United States is becoming ever more litigious. Just as in the public education sector, Lutheran elementary and secondary schools and teachers realize the increasing likelihood of being sued.

In the main, materials published about educational law are oriented toward public schools. The paucity of similar material directed toward the non-public sector puts Lutheran school personnel at a distinct disadvantage, for they too must be wary of court decisions, as well as rules and regulations, that affect their various spheres of service.

This chapter provides information intended to raise the awareness of prospective Lutheran educators in their future dealings with situations that are legally grounded. Where appropriate, suggestions are also provided that may assist in preventing legal problems. The chapter is intended as a basic reference. It does not answer every question related to Lutheran schools and the law.

The law is constantly changing. Many legal aspects are anchored in state law, which differs state by state. Consequently, the Lutheran educator must continually study educational law in his or her state to keep current and should consult with legal authorities at the local and state levels regarding specific situations.

One blessing of American law is the presumption of innocence. People are considered innocent and must be proven guilty. In school law the "burden of proof" is upon those bringing suit. They must, for example, prove the school or the teacher guilty, because the law presumes they are innocent.

THE LEGAL CONTEXT OF LUTHERAN SCHOOLS

In reality, the United States has no "system" of education. Rather, each state has its own method of operating schools. While all states allow Lutheran schools to operate within their boundaries, each has its own approach to controlling them. In some states, such as Michigan, Lutheran schools are strictly regulated. In others, such as Illinois and Nebraska, there is very little regulation of Lutheran schools.

There are several sources of law that influence the operation of Lutheran schools in the United States. Among the most significant are: 1) federal and state constitutions; 2) federal and state statutes; 3) common law; 4) contract law; and 5) tort law.

Federal Constitutional law protects individuals against an infringement of their constitutional freedoms by government or government officials. Since Lutheran schools are not considered governmental agencies and Lutheran educators are not public officials, it may be said that the provisions of the United States Constitution generally do not apply directly to Lutheran schools. Consequently, Lutheran schools may have regulations and procedures that would not be permissible in a public school. Also, it is important to understand that neither students enrolled nor educators serving in Lutheran schools have the same rights as their counterparts in the public school.

Depending on one's perspective, either euphoria or depression could set in regarding Lutheran education's ability to restrict certain freedoms. Before that occurs, it is important to point out that the courts do view Lutheran school students and teachers as persons with rights.

For example, Lutheran school students and teachers could argue that constitutional rights are due them because there exists an intrinsic involvement between the state and the Lutheran school. "State action," as this concept has been called, would need to be so pervasive within the Lutheran school that it could be regarded as a state agent. To date, no student or teacher has been successful in employing the concept against a Lutheran school. In point of fact, receipt of federal and/or state aid, state accreditation, issuance of a state charter, teacher certification, tax exempt status, submitting state forms, and that a Lutheran school is rendering a public function, i.e., education, have all been rejected as arguments constituting a state action.[1] One might argue that Lutheran school involvement in voucher plans and the ensuing probability of increased accountability expectations on the part of government could reverse judicial thinking regarding the concept of state action. As of this writing, however, there is no clear precedent to support such a perspective. As the law is dynamic, one cannot always be sure what the future may hold.

The finding of state action or, additionally, the showing of a compelling state interest are apparently the only two situations where a Lutheran school might be mandated to offer constitutional protections. Case law indicates that without these, Lutheran schools are not bound to the United States Constitution.

The same cannot be said of state constitutions. They may apply as "long as whatever is required does not unfairly impinge upon the rights of [Lutheran] educational institutions and can be shown to have some legitimate educational purpose."[2]

---

[1] Ralph D. Mawdsley, *Legal Problems of Religious and Private Schools* (3rd ed.; Topeka: National Organization on Legal Problems of Education, 1995), 70.

[2] Mary Angela Shaughnessy, *A Primer on School Law: A Guide for Board Members in Catholic Schools* (Washington, D.C.: National Catholic Education Association, 1988), 7.

There are statutory laws at both the federal and state level that specifically do apply to Lutheran elementary and secondary schools. If reasonable, failure to comply with these regulations can result in the imposition of sanctions. However, a compelling state interest in the regulation's enforcement would first have to be demonstrated. Examples of federal laws from this category that do apply to Lutheran schools would be prohibitions of discrimination on the basis of race, sex, handicap, age, and national origin. At the state level, Lutheran schools are generally required to meet student health and safety regulations because the government has a compelling reason for applying them. Even more pervasive in applicability is the agency law formulated by departments of local state government and in local levels of government that directly affect the operation of Lutheran schools.

Common, contract, and tort law are the sources of law most applicable to Lutheran schools, however. It is these three types of law that are the primary focus of this chapter.

Common law "consists of those principles, usage and rules of action applicable to government and security of persons and property that do not rest for their authority upon any positive declaration of the will of the legislature."[3] Common law expects due process or fundamental fairness to exist in the actions of individuals and organizations.

While due process or fairness can be understood from the context of the United States Constitution, we have already pointed out that Lutheran elementary and secondary schools are not bound by it. However, Lutheran schools and the educators that serve in them will be held to standards of fairness consistent with the Lutheran school's principles and "commonly accepted standards of the behavior of reasonable people."[4]

Probably the single most important source of law governing Lutheran schools is contract law. A contract is "[a]n agreement between two or more persons that creates an obligation to do or not to do a particular thing." Generally, the essentials of a contract are that there be

1. competent parties (implying that the parties entering into the contract are lawfully qualified to make the agreement),

2. subject matter (assumes that the provisions of the contract are legal),

3. a legal consideration (what the first party agrees to do for the other party in exchange for something from the second party),

4. mutuality of agreement (implies that two parties entering into a contract agree to its provisions), and

---

[3] Henry Campbell Black, *Black's Law Dictionary* (6th ed.; St. Paul: West Publishing Company, 1990), 276.

[4] Shaughnessy, *A Primer on School Law: A Guide for Board Members in Catholic Schools,* 9.

5. mutuality of obligation (requires that unless both parties to a contract are bound, neither is bound).[5]

If any of these contract essentials is missing, it may be held null and void.

A breach of contract occurs when there is a "[f]ailure, without legal cause, to perform any promise that forms the whole or part of a contract."[6] Within the context of Lutheran education, the breaching party could be the school and/or the administrator, the teacher, the student and/or the parent, or any other party to the contract. Lutheran school teachers' and students' rights and duties are generally contractual. While the school may not opt to include them in the contract, courts place much importance on the development, publication, and implementation of rules and regulations. When expressed in application forms, brochures, catalogs, and handbooks, they can be construed as part of a contractual relationship.

Courts will generally not be concerned with the wisdom, or even the rightness or wrongness, of a Lutheran school's rules and regulations. Their primary concern is "with the existence of a properly promulgated rule or policy and with evidence that the institution acted in good faith according to the procedures it stated would be followed."[7] Courts will scrutinize for fundamental fairness in the contractual relationship between a Lutheran school and the student and/or parent or the teacher when a breach is alleged.

The final source of law that has implications for Lutheran schools is tort law. Many civil suits brought against schools are in the nature of tort suits. A tort provides remedies for private or civil wrongs or injuries independent of contract issues.[8] "[T]he law governing most tort cases in the private sector will not be contract law but will be the same law which is applied in the public school, tort law."[9] Lutheran schools and Lutheran educators can be sued under the tort laws of the state for, among other things, negligent acts that result in injury or loss to the children under their care. While some states grant immunity from tort liability to public school officials in the performance of their official duties, such immunities generally do not apply to Lutheran school officials since they are not considered state officers. The somewhat similar doctrine of charitable immunity could have possibly been utilized successfully by Lutheran schools in the past, but since World War II the doctrine has been largely nullified.[10] Case law appears to

---

[5] Black, *Black's Law Dictionary*, 322.

[6] Black, *Black's Law Dictionary*, 188.

[7] Shaughnessy, *A Primer on School Law: A Guide for Board Members in Catholic Schools*, 13.

[8] Black, *Black's Law Dictionary*, 1489.

[9] Shaughnessy, *A Primer on School Law: A Guide for Board Members in Catholic Schools*, 15.

[10] Mawdsley, *Legal Problems of Religious and Private Schools*, 1.

indicate that Lutheran educators are required to extend "the same degree of care a reasonable person or group of persons would exercise."[11]

As should be apparent, the operation of Lutheran schools is both supported and limited by a wide variety of legal structures. We now turn to the subject of the Lutheran teacher's rights and duties under the law.

The Lutheran School Teacher's Rights and Responsibilities

Case law has clarified some of the rights and duties of Lutheran educators in carrying out their service. In addition, many of the rights and duties have been written into the law.

Testing and Investigation of Applicants for Certification and Employment

In many, though not all, Lutheran schools, teachers desiring to serve are required to possess teaching certificates usually issued by the state. Many states require background checks for teacher certification or employment. Generally, these checks have gone unchallenged.

Obviously, if the requirements would extend to drug testing, the issue becomes much more controversial. Lower federal and state courts have rejected such tests for public school employees unless reasonable suspicion of illegal drug use can be shown. Since Lutheran teachers are not considered public officials, the Constitutional Fourth Amendment applicability of these cases has little consequence, especially if a Lutheran school has a requirement for drug testing of prospective or current faculty.

Nearly all states require prospective teachers to pass one or more competency tests for certification. Most lawsuits charging that these tests are discriminatory either have not been successful or have been withdrawn because the available data did not demonstrate a clear pattern of discrimination.

Employment Contracts, Tenure, and Due Process in Dismissal

The rights of Lutheran teachers are generally conferred by contracts or agreements existing between the teacher and the Lutheran school. Whether these are classified as tenured calls, nontenured calls, or simply contracts and/or agreements, contract law governs the employment situation.

State statutes may confer additional rights as well. Teachers may be said to hold rights under the common law. Although the concept of common law

---

[11] Shaughnessy, *A Primer on School Law: A Guide for Board Members in Catholic Schools*, 16.

rights is obvious in theory, it is somewhat more difficult to delineate in legal practice. What may seem to be a principle of common law to one person may not seem so to another. One person may consider it immoral to dismiss a teacher for freely speaking his or her mind about administrative practices; another may deem dismissing a teacher for such a reason as perfectly acceptable and, indeed, courts have upheld such dismissals.[12]

A decision to dismiss a Lutheran teacher from a call, tenured or nontenured, or a contract is not to be made lightly. When a decision is made, the Lutheran school must proceed according to the policies in place.

Courts will scrutinize the tenured or nontenured call or the contract to insure that the provisions contained therein have been followed. As indicated above, courts will also scrutinize handbooks and policy statements as part of the contractual relationship and hold Lutheran schools to their provisions. In this regard, it is important to point out that the constitution of The Lutheran Church—Missouri Synod contains provisions that relate to the termination of called teachers.[13]

It is also helpful to be familiar with laws governing the dismissal of teachers in the public sector. They may be of assistance in policy development for Lutheran schools that would reflect fundamental fairness. At a minimum, these policies should ask for extensive and complete documentation of all evidence supporting a decision to dismiss a Lutheran teacher from a call, tenured or nontenured, or contract.

Just as Lutheran schools are bound to the terms of a contract, so too are the Lutheran teachers serving under a tenured or nontenured call or an employment agreement. Not complying with the terms of the called or contractual relationship can be the basis for dismissal, and courts have upheld dismissals based on such noncompliance.

While Lutheran schools have the discretion of offering tenure, "courts will scrutinize the policies of an institution which does not have a formal tenure policy to see if there is an informal or formal policy in existence such that *de facto* (tenure in fact) exists." If a Lutheran school does not extend tenure to teachers via either the divine call or other employment agreements, "it should clearly state in a policy or handbook that there is no tenure/expectation that employment will continue beyond a given contract year."[14]

Lutheran teachers, either called or contracted, may be legitimately dismissed if enrollment declines or financial constraints are present. It is not uncommon for Lutheran schools to confront the need for *reduction in force* (RIF). It is strongly

---

[12] Shaughnessy, *A Primer on School Law: A Guide for Board Members in Catholic Schools*, 24–25.

[13] See Article VI, 3 and Article XII, 7–8 as well as procedures set forth in the Bylaws of the Synod.

[14] Shaughnessy, *A Primer on School Law: A Guide for Board Members in Catholic Schools*, 26.

recommended that RIF policies and procedures be in place prior to deciding to reduce staff, however.

Lutheran schools may not cloak themselves with separation of church and state protections emanating from the First Amendment and then proceed with any actions they wish to take. Courts will exercise jurisdiction over contracts made between a Lutheran school and a teacher, particularly regarding issues unrelated to doctrine.

That Lutheran schools are not considered to be state actors is because its employment relationships are governed by contract as opposed to federal and state constitutions. Consequently, constitutional standards such as due process are not required of Lutheran schools in their employment relationships. However, litigants may introduce them in seeking to enforce contractual terms. While Lutheran schools may not have to meet constitutional standards of due process in dealing with their employees, courts have displayed a willingness to require a general sense of basic fairness, e.g., expecting that a Lutheran teacher would be able to hear and answer charges. Thus, called and contracted teachers in Lutheran schools have rights that should be protected.

PROTECTION AGAINST ASSAULT

The problem of physical assault on teachers has increased in recent decades. Courts generally convict defendants who violate either educational statutes or state criminal codes. Lutheran educators can help protect themselves and their colleagues by vigorously pressing criminal charges and initiating civil suits for assault and battery.

SELF-DEFENSE AND RESTRAINT

Since, unfortunately, Lutheran schools are not immune to violence, school personnel need to understand the parameters surrounding the use of physical force for self-defense or the restraint of pupils. As in so many areas of school law, the standard of reasonableness is used to evaluate the amount of force Lutheran teachers may use to defend themselves or to restrain students. The courts seem willing to uphold the educator so long as the bounds of reasonableness are followed.

In self-defense situations, the amount of force deemed reasonable would probably be contingent upon "the age of the pupil, the nature of the attacker's action necessitating defense, and the action of the one attacked after the attack has ceased."[15] As a norm, the amount of force used to defend oneself should be commensurate with the amount of force used by the one doing the attacking.

---

[15] Steve P. Permuth, Ralph D. Mawdsley, and Joseph Daly, *The Law, the Student, and the Catholic School* (Washington, D.C.: National Catholic Education Association, 1981), 48.

In order to justify the use of force on the ground of self-defense, it is not required to show that the use of force was necessary to protect from imminent personal injury. It is sufficient if the necessity was real or apparent. But the mere belief of the person attacked is not sufficient to justify the use of force.[16]

The use of restraint by Lutheran school personnel is probably more common than self-defense. The most obvious school situation calling for restraint is a fight between students. Because of the possible harm to the participants as well as the spectators, various states provide the educator, either through statute or common law, with a mandated duty to attempt to stop the fight and to protect the combatants and others, up to the ability of the educator. If the altercation cannot be stopped by physical restraint, the Lutheran educator should immediately seek other help and also inform the administration.

As with self-defense, the standard of reasonableness is the key to avoiding liability. It would appear that so long as the Lutheran educator focuses on separating the fighting students and does not champion the cause of one or the other combatants, no liability risk for injuries would exist.

VERBAL ABUSE OF STUDENTS

Since Lutheran schools are not state agents, a discussion of such constitutional rights as freedom of expression is moot. However, a Lutheran teacher is expected to know the difference between verbally encouraging and belittling a student in the classroom. A tort action for intentional infliction of emotional distress may follow an outburst by a frustrated Lutheran teacher who so ridicules and belittles a student in front of the other students that the student is not only defamed but is impeded from intellectual and personal growth. If a student suffers physically from that distress, his or her case may be even stronger in court.

ACADEMIC FREEDOM AND TEACHER AS ROLE MODEL

Academic freedom refers to the teacher's freedom to choose subject matter and instructional materials relevant to the classroom without interference from administrators or outsiders. In most Lutheran schools, curriculum development is a matter of collegial cooperation, and teaching in accordance with the curriculum as ultimately constituted is a Lutheran teacher's called or contractual duty. To a large degree, however, Lutheran school curriculum content and instructional materials are controlled by forces other than the First Amendment of the United States Constitution. Whereas public school boards may not exercise an individual member's prejudice and personal taste in limiting academic freedom, the called or contracted Lutheran teacher's so-called academic freedom is limit-

---

[16] Permuth, Mawdsley, and Daly, *The Law, the Student, and the Catholic School*, 49.

ed by the religious and confessional nature and ends of the Lutheran elementary or secondary school.

Even in activities outside the school, a Lutheran teacher's expression of beliefs may be limited by the Synod's doctrinal position. Case law indicates that a Lutheran school teacher could be dismissed even though he or she was exercising free speech rights.[17] Also, engaging in certain gross behaviors that may be deemed "unbecoming a teacher," and even though occurring off campus, may result in the termination of a Lutheran teacher. Fundamental fairness should still be adhered to, however.

TORT LIABILITY AND NEGLIGENCE

Negligence is one type of a more formal legal concept called tort. A tort is an actionable wrong that the law will recognize and set right. Negligence is doing something that a reasonable, prudent teacher would not have done in like or similar circumstances or not doing something that a reasonable, prudent teacher would have done in like or similar circumstances where the teacher had a duty. Simply, a Lutheran school or teacher may be judged negligent either for an improper act or for not acting properly. Most school lawsuits relate to negligence.

In determining a cause of action for negligence, the same formula that is applicable in public education also applies to Lutheran schools and their personnel. This formula may be viewed as a four-link chain as illustrated below:

The first link, duty, requires Lutheran school personnel to meet a certain standard of conducting themselves for the protection of their students from unreasonable risks. A school's duty frequently is determined by policy. Every official school policy must be carried out by the school.

Lutheran educators should be aware that both written and unwritten policies of the school may become duties or standards against which their conduct may be measured. Any deviation from such policies of the school may be viewed as a breach of the duty of the educator.

The second link, breach, focuses on whether the Lutheran teacher breached or violated one of his or her duties. Pivotal here is whether the risk at hand was foreseeable by a reasonable person in like or similar circumstances.

Causation, commonly known as "legal cause" or "proximate cause," the third link of the negligence chain formula, may be the most difficult to apply because

---

[17] Mawdsley, *Legal Problems of Religious and Private Schools*, 72.

there must exist a reasonably close causal connection between the conduct and the resulting injury. For example, who would be liable—the teacher who sent a responsible fourth-grade student on an errand two blocks away from campus during the school day or the driver of a speeding vehicle who ran a red light and seriously injured the fourth-grade student? While the teacher may be remiss in his or her duty to supervise, the negligence of the driver of the vehicle is the proximate cause of the injuries sustained by the student. Therefore the driver, not the teacher, probably would be found liable, although in many cases there are multiple defendants.

The final link, injury, can be thought of as the actual loss or damage resulting to the interest of another. Case law indicates that the injury "is to be physical in nature."[18] However, there could be suits for physical effects or emotional injury.

It is important to remember that each element of the formula must be present. If any link of the so-called negligence chain is broken, negligence cannot be proven.

It should also be pointed out that relying on exculpatory language through the use of waivers for field trips, travel, and other matters as a means of circumventing a tort action is ill-advised. Release and waiver forms signed by minor children releasing their own rights or parents or guardians releasing their children's rights are of questionable legal value.

Release and waiver forms signed by minors are simply of no validity. Assuming the forms are exceptionally well written and contain the appropriate language and warnings, there is operative a presupposition that some parents or guardians will not sue for minor injuries because they think they may be blocked by the execution of release forms. Release forms will not, however, prevent parents or guardians, on the advice of legal counsel, from suing when the child is seriously injured.

Even if the student is of adult status and emancipated, the Lutheran educator's failure to observe a standard of conduct that then is a proximate cause of an injury to a member of a class of people who are to be protected in his or her supervisory or disciplinary capacity cannot easily, if at all, be waived for failure to observe appropriate standards of conduct, especially with students. While not set in stone for adults who waive rights, the value of waivers for adults is also highly questionable.

Reporting Child Abuse

Nearly every state requires both public and non-public school personnel to report suspected child abuse. In addition, some state statutes specify to whom the abuse is to be reported. Normally the local child-welfare unit is the designated body.

---

[18] Permuth, Mawdsley, and Daly, *The Law, the Student, and the Catholic School*, 14.

In matters of child abuse, Lutheran school personnel should be cognizant of the following:

1. Child abuse and child abuse reporting statutes apply equally to the public and private sectors. There is no exemption for nonpublic schools.

2. Almost all child abuse reporting statutes do not permit school personnel to exercise their judgment in deciding whether marks or injuries resulting from other than accidental means constitute child abuse. Apparently only social services personnel are permitted to make such a determination.

3. A legislative policy mandating reporting cannot be subverted by a school's internal administrative policies. It is not unusual for schools to have a written or unwritten policy that school personnel are to report cases of alleged child abuse to a designated administrative official. Subordinate school personnel, if mandated to report by state statute, need to be aware that reporting suspected child abuse to a school administrator does not excuse them from their statutory responsibility if the administrator fails or refuses to notify social services.

4. Any school personnel whose names are reported for suspected child abuse should act promptly to protect themselves and contact an attorney prior to granting an interview to a social services representative. Waiting until trial to engage legal counsel may jeopardize one's case if damaging admissions have already been made.[19]

It might also be noted that neither delegation of authority to spank nor consent to spank are valid defenses in a criminal prosecution for child abuse, based upon the concept that no parent can consent to child abuse.

EDUCATIONAL MALPRACTICE

To date, the term "educational malpractice" has not been recognized as actionable, thereby permitting disgruntled parents or students to sue Lutheran schools. The problems involving malpractice cases may be summarized as follows: 1) no standard of care can be determined; 2) uncertainty as to the reasons for failure to learn and the determination of monetary damages; 3) the potential for a flood of similar litigation; and 4) courts involving themselves with the daily operation of schools.

COPYRIGHT LAWS

The widespread use of copying machines has bred serious and regular violations of copyright laws. Lutheran school teachers should be aware that photo-

---

[19] Mawdsley, *Legal Problems of Religious and Private Schools*, 50.

copying is governed—ambiguously to be sure—by the "fair use doctrine" reflected in the 1976 Copyright Law. This law amended the original 1909 copyright laws to include photocopying and the educational use of copyrighted materials.

Whether copied materials violate the fair use doctrine is tested by such points as the purpose for which copies are made, the nature of the work copied, the amount of the work copied, and the potential impact on the publisher's market. The following is a summary of fair use restrictions on copying materials for educational use:

1. Copying of prose is limited to excerpts of no more than 1,000 words.

2. Copies from an anthology or encyclopedia cannot exceed one story or entry, or 2,500 words.

3. A poem may be copied if it is less than 250 words, and an excerpt of no more then 250 words may be copied from a longer poem.

4. Distribution of copies from the same author more than once a semester or copying from the same work or anthology more than three times during the semester is prohibited.

5. Teachers may make one copy per student for class distribution; if charges are made, they may not exceed actual copying costs.

6. It is illegal to create anthologies or compilations by using photocopies as a substitute for purchasing the same or similar materials.

7. Consumable materials, such as workbooks, may not be copied.

8. Under the fair use doctrine, single copies of printed materials may be made for personal study, lesson planning, research, criticism, comment, and news reporting.

9. Most magazine and newspaper articles may be copied freely. However, items in weekly newspapers and magazines designed for classroom use by students may not be copied without permission.

10. Individual teachers must decide, independently, to copy material; they may not be directed to do so by higher authorities.

11. There are three categories of material for which copies may be freely made: writings published before 1978 that have never been copyrighted, published works for which copyrights are more than seventy-five years old, and U.S. government publications.

12. New restrictions on the use of copyrighted materials are emerging in connection with the Internet and other digital media.[20]

---

[20] Alan C. Ornstein and Daniel U. Levine, *Foundations of Education* (7th ed.; Boston: Houghton Mifflin Company, 2000), 245.

The legal way to reproduce copyrighted materials is to obtain permission from the copyright holder. This approach is also recommended if copies of materials in books that have been declared "out of print" are needed as well as for Lutheran school presentations of copyrighted plays and musical productions. Generally, a letter addressed to the permissions department of the copyrighted work's publisher begins the process. The Lutheran school may need to pay royalties on performances, sometimes the amount being contingent upon whether or not admission is charged.

Videotapes and computer software are also subject to the same fair use guidelines as other copyrighted materials. The scope of this chapter does not permit further treatment, but helpful resources are available to assist Lutheran educators in this sphere.[21]

The foregoing has provided an overview of some significant areas containing rights and duties under the law impacting the Lutheran educator. We now turn to the subject of the legal rights and duties of students enrolled in Lutheran schools.

Student Rights and Duties in the Lutheran School

Much of the conflict and case law regarding student rights in public schools over the past several decades has evolved because the courts have employed standards of constitutional restraint upon public school officials. Lutheran schools do not function under those same constitutional norms because, as previously pointed out, they are not considered to be agencies of the state. Consequently, constitutional rights such as due process or freedom of expression may not be applicable to students enrolled in Lutheran schools.

In fact, one court made the following distinctions between not only Lutheran schools but also all private schools over against their public counterparts:

1. Private schools perform a valuable social function by providing diversity that the government may not and should not provide in public schools.

2. Because it is nongovernmental, private education is not restricted to the same nonpartisan and secular goals as is public education.

3. Private schools may provide religious instruction, propagate a sectarian viewpoint, and conduct religious services, which public schools may not.

4. Private schools may emphasize moral development and strict discipline in ways that public schools may not.

---

[21] See, for example, *The Copyright Primer for Librarians and Educators* by Mary Hutchings Reed. This joint publication of the American Library Association and the National Education Association is well-organized and easy to read. See also the Copyright Management Center's website, http://www.iupui.edu/~copyinfo/ and the Stanford University Libraries website, http://fairuse.stanford.edu/.

5. Private schools may discourage criticism and irreverence toward existing institutions or policies, which public schools may not.

6. Private schools may impose discipline in conformity of dress, speech, and action, which public schools may not.[22]

Lest Lutheran educators become too smug in perusing this list, as was already indicated earlier in this chapter, courts do not view Lutheran school students as persons without any rights at all.

As was also alluded to earlier, probably the single most important source of rights and duties for those enrolled in Lutheran schools stems from the contractual relationship between the school, parents or guardians, and students. While a Lutheran school may choose not to include them in the contract, rules and regulations governing student behavior that are stated in application forms, brochures, catalogs, and handbooks create both expressed and implied expectations for the student, the parent or guardian, and the institution.[23] Generally, the student attends a Lutheran school with the expectation that compliance with its rules (both written and unwritten) and customs is required. The Lutheran school is also required to comply with its written requirements and procedures concerning students. If, for example, the Lutheran school offers certain due process rights, e.g., notice and hearing, in its published materials, then it must grant them.

FREEDOM OF EXPRESSION

The First Amendment provides for free speech and a free press. The lack of employment of the state action standard excuses the Lutheran school from extending these basic constitutional rights usually found in its public counterpart.

As a result, students enrolled in Lutheran elementary and secondary schools do not have the constitutionally protected right to express themselves via the spoken or written word. Rather, their freedom is controlled by the contractual relationship between child or parent or guardian and the school. Specific contractual provisions are found in handbooks, applications, and brochures that usually impose limitations upon student expression that are consistent with the tenets of The Lutheran Church—Missouri Synod. There appear to be no constitutional restraints upon these limitations. However, if a Lutheran school extends certain rights in a handbook relating to speech and publications or to procedural fairness, it must honor them.

Parents or guardians could intervene on behalf of the child where the disciplinary consequence of violating a Lutheran school's speech and publication regulations was unfair or resulted in expulsion.

---

[22] Permuth, Mawdsley, and Daly, *The Law, the Student, and the Catholic School*, 3.

[23] Mawdsley, *Legal Problems of Religious and Private Schools*, 65.

DRESS CODES AND REGULATIONS

Because Lutheran schools are not literally bound by public school case law, dress and grooming rules and regulations are also at their discretion. As with other policies, rules about personal appearance usually are found in the parent and/or student handbook. And again, such rules and regulations possess a contractual quality in defining the relationship between student, parent or guardian, and the Lutheran school and "any procedural rights granted in the school literature must be afforded before final disciplinary action."[24]

In a Lutheran school, dress codes and haircut requirements may be quite general or extremely specific. Public school requirements probably would have to be based on showing a specific school interest, e.g., health, safety. In Lutheran schools this would not be the case.

This sizable grant of freedom is premised, in part, on the idea that attendance in a Lutheran school is not required by state law. Consequently, parents or guardians voluntarily send their children and, therefore, consent to the published personal appearance rules of the Lutheran school. If the parent or guardian does not agree with those rules, they are free to enroll the child elsewhere, with the child not being totally removed from the educative process.

The courts would probably require a minimum standard of fairness, should expulsion be the consequence for violating a Lutheran school's personal appearance code. Simply allowing the student the opportunity to tell his or her side of the story would appear to be sufficient in meeting this standard.

SUSPENSION AND EXPULSION

According to interpretations of the Federal Constitution, all children have the right to an education. However, they do not have a right to an education in a Lutheran school.

If the Lutheran school has adopted written or oral policies regarding suspension and expulsion of students, these same policies must apply to all children. No student may be removed on the basis of special or unique requirements or expectations for that child alone. In all events, all children must be treated fairly.

Because Lutheran schools are not considered to be agencies of the state, constitutional due process procedures are not expected of them. However, since public school law is sometimes considered precedent for non-public schools, Lutheran schools may wish to follow procedures required of public schools regarding suspensions and expulsions in their specific state.

Expulsion should be done only by the parish or school's board of education, certainly not by a teacher nor by an administrator. If requested, the student should have a right to a hearing before the board.

---

[24] Permuth, Mawdsley, and Daly, *The Law, the Student, and the Catholic School*, 36.

As long as federal statutes are not violated, individual states could make their laws more stringent. Therefore, the following suggestions should also be considered in carrying out suspension and expulsion:

1. Publish school regulations regarding student offenses that might lead to suspension and/or expulsion.

2. Notify students of their "rights" (as determined by the [Lutheran] school) under suspension and expulsion.

3. Understand that, even under public school law, emergency suspensions are clearly permissible in cases of immediate threat to school property, but that even emergency suspensions should immediately be followed by appropriate hearings, etc., once the danger is no longer existent.

4. Carefully document all information (regardless of time dimension) that may need to be brought forth and do it as objectively as possible.[25]

Search and Seizure

The Fourth Amendment to the United States Constitution provides guarantees against unreasonable search and seizure. Since the concept of state action has yet to be employed against a Lutheran school, it is highly doubtful that the reasonableness in suspicion and scope standard applied to public schools is applicable to Lutheran schools.

Consequently, unless limited by a contract or handbook clause, Lutheran school personnel may enter a student's desk or locker "at any time to search for contraband. Such searches can be unannounced and selective, and they can be done even if there has been no report of wrongdoing."[26] If contraband is found, the Lutheran school student would be subject not only to in-house discipline consequences, but if the contraband also violated state law, e.g., controlled substances, he or she could also be involved in criminal action because the evidence would be admissible "without judicial scrutiny as to the reason for the search."[27] Simply, a Lutheran school does not have to have a reason for a desk or locker search.

However, the fact that the Lutheran school provides students with desks and/or lockers

> would appear to make the school a bailee of the student's locker contents. If, during the course of a locker search, a student's property is damaged or missing through an absence of ordinary care by the school, the school would be liable to make restitution.[28]

---

[25] Permuth, Mawdsley, and Daly, *The Law, the Student, and the Catholic School*, 78.

[26] Permuth, Mawdsley, and Daly, *The Law, the Student, and the Catholic School*, 63.

[27] Permuth, Mawdsley, and Daly, *The Law, the Student, and the Catholic School*, 63.

[28] Permuth, Mawdsley, and Daly, *The Law, the Student, and the Catholic School*, 63.

Desk and locker searches that commandeer student property that is prohibited only by a school regulation could result in an intentional tort called "trespass to personal property." Those items of student personal property that may have been seized by the teacher because of related misbehavior, e.g., squirt guns, comic books, toy cars, remain the property of the student unless the item is illegal. Because the contractual relationship between the student, the parent or guardian, and the Lutheran school terminates at the end of the school year, it would be advisable to return these items to the student, or to the parent or guardian, no later than the last day of school.

Searches of a student's person present complexities not found in desk and locker searches. Tort action for assault and battery and invasion of privacy could be the direct result, especially if a student is strip searched. Consequently, any search of a student's person conducted by Lutheran educators should be sensitive to the standard of the reasonable and prudent teacher in like and similar circumstances. Implicit here would be the reasonableness of initiating the search as well as its intrusiveness.

CLASSROOM DISCIPLINE AND CORPORAL PUNISHMENT

If one were forced to select a cornerstone concept within the context of school law, *in loco parentis* (in place of the parents) would quite probably be chosen. The concept assumes a managerial dimension that says that, like parents, school personnel possess the right to discipline children in their care. Therefore educators may formulate rules and regulations that govern student behavior, regulate misbehavior, secure compliance, decide guilt or innocence, and mete out punishment. Legally, it appears that Lutheran educators stand in the place of parents. However, like their public school counterparts, they do not have unlimited jurisdiction and are limited to educational pursuits.

Some states prohibit corporal punishment in either public or nonpublic schools, while others do not. On the basis of state statute, it appears that Lutheran school personnel may employ corporal punishment as a consequence for unacceptable student behavior. However, even in states that permit or do not directly prohibit it, damages or criminal conviction for assault and battery could be leveled against the Lutheran educator for what is deemed harsh or excessive physical punishment.

In some instances Lutheran schools receive written permission from parents or guardians to use corporal punishment. Sometimes this is a statement on an enrollment or application form or on an individual consent form. While this is generally good practice, it should be remembered that a parent or guardian does not consent to unreasonable punishment being directed toward the child.

The use of corporal punishment is discouraged because other disciplinary procedures often produce better results and because of the possibility of negative legal consequences. If the Lutheran school believes that the use of corporal punishment is helpful in carrying out its management function, the following suggestions may assist in preventing civil or criminal action:

1. In advance provide students and parents with information about the kinds of conduct that may result in corporal punishment;

2. Use corporal punishment as a last resort, with emphasis being on alternative means of changing behavior;

3. Investigate any denial of guilt prior to administering corporal punishment;

4. Designate only one person in the school to administer the punishment;

5. Have a witness present;

6. Limit punishment to no more than three swats.[29]

SEXUAL HARASSMENT OR MOLESTATION OF STUDENTS

Definitions of these terms vary, but for interactions between students and teachers the terms generally include not only sexual contact that calls into question the teacher's role as exemplar but also unwelcome sexual advances or requests for favors, particularly when the recipient may believe that refusal will affect his or her academic standing. Sexual abuse or harassment of one student by another is also subsumed under these terms.

Possible sources for litigation involving Lutheran schools are statutory emanating from Title IX of the Education Amendments of 1972 and Section 1983 of the 1964 Civil Rights Act. Title IX addresses employee-to-employee, employee-to-student, and student-to-student relationships. Under Section 1983, school officials can be held liable for supervisory failures that result in the molestation of a school child if those failures manifest a deliberate indifference to the constitutional rights of the child.

Under the current status of the law, Title IX and Section 1983 are not equally applicable to Lutheran schools. Title IX will be applicable to Lutheran schools only if they receive assistance administered by the United States Department of Education. However, Section 1983 would not apply to Lutheran schools unless there has been state action.[30]

Lutheran schools that receive, or plan to receive, federal funds should disseminate a sexual harassment policy and procedure. They would be held liable for damages only if school officials had knowledge of, and were deliberately indifferent to, sexual harassment among students or, for that matter, others on campus. The harassment would need to be so severe, widespread, and objectively offensive that it would prevent the victim access to the educational opportunities or benefits provided by the Lutheran school.

---

[29] Mawdsley, *Legal Problems of Religious and Private Schools*, 44–45.

[30] Mawdsley, *Legal Problems of Religious and Private Schools*, 144–146.

STUDENT RECORDS AND PRIVACY ACTS

The Family Educational Rights and Privacy Act of 1974 increased students' and parents' or guardians' access to school records and restricted the availability of school record information to third parties. In addition, it provided parents or guardians the right to challenge the content of school records. Any school receiving federal assistance administered by the United States Department of Education is bound to adhere to the provisions of the act.

Student records present the Lutheran school or educator with possible legal hazards. They include:

1. defamation if the information in the record is false;

2. invasion of privacy for releasing information to unauthorized third parties;

3. infliction of mental distress; for example, calling a child "a high grade moron";

4. a court order to expunge illegal or inaccurate records;

5. a court order enjoining dissemination of adverse student records.[31]

It would be prudent for Lutheran educators to follow student record statutes applicable to public schools in their states. While these mandates might not be required of the Lutheran school, concern for privacy, confidentiality, justice, and fairness should be a significant part of the Lutheran educational experience, regardless of legislative mandate or legal interpretation.

SUMMING UP

It should be apparent even to the casual reader that the operation of Lutheran schools is both supported and limited by a wide variety of legal frameworks. These structures impact both those who serve and are enrolled in Lutheran elementary and secondary schools.

The purpose of this chapter was to raise the level of awareness of Lutheran educators in the area of educational law. Ultimately, the Lutheran educator should be practicing preventive law.

DISCUSSION TOPICS AND SUGGESTED PROJECTS

1. As indicated in chapter 2, *Meyer v. Nebraska* (1923) and *Pierce v. Society of Sisters* (1925) guaranteed Lutheran schools the right to carry on educational endeavors so long as they met the necessary state requirements and objectives. Trace these landmark cases from the trial court stage through the United States Supreme Court decision. What questions were raised? What

---

[31] Permuth, Mawdsley, and Daly, *The Law, the Student, and the Catholic School*, 60.

defense was offered? What reasons did judges at the various levels give for their decisions? What were the constitutional implications of the case?

2. What are the costs and benefits of a Lutheran school awarding tenure? For whom?

3. Lutheran teachers do not have constitutional free speech rights. What might be the costs and benefits of permitting them the right of free speech? For whom? What limitations may be most justifiable?

4. From a nearby Lutheran school, collect and analyze information about teachers' responsibilities for identifying and reporting child abuse. What are the school's explicit policies. Have any teachers been released or otherwise disciplined for failure to meet these responsibilities?

5. Ask someone who teaches a school law course at your university to come to class to discuss Lutheran teachers' rights and duties.

6. Invite a principal from a local Lutheran school to come in and discuss how that school deals with the student rights and duties outlined in the chapter. Obtain copies of the school's handbooks, if possible.

7. Should the due process rights of students in Lutheran schools differ from those in public schools? Why or why not? What differences may be most justifiable?

RESOURCES, INFLUENCES, AND SUGGESTED FURTHER READING

Black, Henry Campbell. *Black's Law Dictionary*. 6th ed. St. Paul: West Publishing Company, 1990.

Furst, Lyndon G., and Charles J. Russo. *The Legal Aspects of Nonpublic Schools: A Casebook*. Berrien Springs, Michigan: Andrews University Press, 1993.

Hammar, Richard R. "Administration of Private Schools." Pages 679–725 in *Pastor, Church and Law*. 2nd ed. Matthews, North Carolina: Christian Ministry Resources, 1991.

Mawdsley, Ralph. *Legal Problems of Religious and Private Schools*. 3rd ed. Topeka: National Organization on Legal Problems of Education, 1995.

Ornstein, Allan C., and Daniel U. Levine. *Foundations of Education*. 7th ed. Boston: Houghton Mifflin Company, 2000.

Permuth, Steve P., Ralph D. Mawdsley, and Joseph Daly. *The Law, the Student, and the Catholic School*. Washington, D.C.: National Catholic Education Association, 1981.

Rietschel, William C. *Give to Caesar: Lutheran Schools and Government Law*. St. Louis: Department of School Ministry, The Lutheran Church—Missouri Synod, 1999.

Saalfield, Albrecht. *A Legal Primer for Independent Schools*. Boston: National Association for Independent Schools, 1983.

Shaughnessy, Mary Angela. *A Primer on School Law: A Guide for Board Members in Catholic Schools*. Washington, D.C.: National Catholic Education Association, 1988.

9

LUTHERAN EDUCATION
IN A CHANGING WORLD

This concluding chapter identifies various current social trends and suggests some possible implications of these trends for Lutheran schools. It attempts to predict the future on the basis of these trends and on the basis of historical evidence.

In order to plan for the journey through our new millennium, we must first attempt to describe it. Lutheran teachers will need to help their students be competent, contributing, faithful Christian adults in this new century, just as they did in the past. Lutheran schools must continue to provide vibrant, effective ministry in the twenty-first century.

Several of the previous chapters identified changes that have occurred over time. For example, Lutheran schools have gradually blended into the American mainstream and now serve a constituency that has greatly changed over the years. The traditionally narrow Lutheran school focus on nurturing its own in teaching the faith has been broadened with a biblical theology of mission. The synodical placement process for teachers has changed. And our world continues to change. As part of that world, Lutheran schools will also continue to change. The concept of village and camp may assist the Lutheran teacher in understanding current social trends and the inevitable change that accompanies them.

THE VILLAGE AND THE CAMP

The roots of the Lutheran church lie largely in northern European villages. Geographical boundaries defined these villages so that it was relatively easy to determine who was included in the community and who was not.

Relationships developed within the village; central to the village was the church. If you were born in the village, you were born into the church. In some European countries, the church still keeps the birth records for the community. The people of the village formed a homogeneous community, one big related family. All knew one another. When it gathered for worship, the church assumed that family-type relationships existed, an assumption that was reflected in the formal structure of the worship. The strong sense of family undergirded the village, just as it supported the ministry of the church.

The Lutheran church transplanted the village concept when it arrived in the United States. The borders of the new village may not have been geographical, but new boundaries were based on culture, ethnicity, and language. If you could speak German, Norwegian, or Swedish, you were accepted in one of the Lutheran villages. As alluded to in chapter 2, language and culture were significant and certainly contributed to the Missouri Synod's identity as a community. A strong sense of extended family supported the church's ministry.

The concept of the camp is very different from that of the village. In the frontier camp of the Old West, there was no permanent or stable sense of community. Each night a community of sorts was formed as camp members gathered around the campfire to tell stories, sing ballads, or join together in worship. There was no permanent church building. The fluidity and mobility of people affected family and church.

While the concept of village and camp[1] may certainly serve as a guide for understanding current trends, there is also a need for a caveat here. Lutheran teachers should be cautioned that their assumption of either village or camp influences how they understand and respond to changes in society, changes that are moving us farther away from the village and closer to the camp.

TRENDS THAT AFFECT LUTHERAN SCHOOL MINISTRY

Among the several significant trends that will affect Lutheran schools in this new millennium are an aging population, a shrinking world, and changes in families, values, technology, and education. These trends do not comprise a complete list, nor are the descriptions that accompany them exhaustive, but rather are provided to assist the prospective Lutheran teacher in developing a new understanding of the scope and style of the future ministry of Lutheran schools.

CHANGING FAMILIES

In the village, the traditional nuclear family consisted of the husband/father—wage earner, wife/mother—homemaker, and two to five children. Today, the "family" is changing. We are developing a new vocabulary in our attempt to define and describe the family and its changing nature. For example,

Single-parent families. Most children will live with only one parent for some time before age 18. Usually women are the custodial parent. Most single parent "moms" have limited economic means. The role of the noncustodial parent in the child's education is a question mark for most educators.

---

[1] David Luecke developed the concept of village and camp in *Evangelical Style and Lutheran Substance: Facing America's Mission Challenge* (St. Louis: Concordia Publishing House, 1988).

Blended families. Remarriage often combines families. Children today can have more parents than parents have children. Blended families, families that result from remarriages, face many difficulties.

Grandparent families. Some grandparents, especially grandmothers, are now parenting their grandchildren because the parents cannot or will not accept that responsibility. Causes vary, from accidental death or sickness to immaturity or substance abuse.

DINK families (double income, no kids). Some couples decide not to have children. Others intentionally delay having children until they are established in a career. Society seems to accept couples who live together out of wedlock. "Partner" is replacing "spouse" in our vocabulary. The average age for first marriage is increasing for both males and females.

Transformational families. Some families are headed by older divorced or widowed women. Women share the family responsibilities for social and economic reasons.

Gay and lesbian families. Gay and lesbian couples sometimes raise children from former marriages, adopt children, or raise foster children. In some instances, lesbian couples have utilized artificial insemination to conceive, and then raise a child.

Parenthood II families. Some adult children live with their parents after they have finished college. Adult children return because they are unable to earn enough to live on their own and pay off their college debts. This arrangement fills the empty nest again for the parents and creates a new role for both parents and the adult child.

Two-generation retired families. Retired parents may live with retired adult children.

Gangs. Youth join gangs as a family substitute. There they find acceptance, identity, and a sense of family (brotherhood/sisterhood). The gang shapes their identity and controls their behavior, much as a family would.

Singles. More and more adults choose never to marry or cohabitate.

Many of these "family" styles are not new. Today they are receiving legal status and social recognition. The traditional nuclear family still exists, but it is less common than formerly.

The implications of changing families for the twenty-first century Lutheran school are many. Certainly the Lutheran school will minister to diverse family structures and styles. The need for after-school care for children of working parents will increase. The traditional relationship between school and home, parents and teachers will continue to change. Parents will have less time for meeting with teachers, assisting in the classroom, and monitoring homework. Lutheran schools will have to continue to help students and parents develop good communication and problem-solving skills. Can you think of other implications for the Lutheran school?

Aging Population

Not long ago the phrase "Don't trust anyone over 30" was popular. Today, the phrase is reversed and is "Don't trust anyone under 30." The population of the United States is aging. Consequently, the median age of the United States population increased steadily during the last half of the twentieth century and conventional wisdom appears to assume that this trend will continue well into the twenty-first century.

Lutheran schools will need to provide services for aged people. For example, Lutheran schools might develop older adult enrichment programs for personal growth and fulfillment. The growing pool of older adults provides a new source of talent for paraprofessional roles in the school. Many Lutheran schools have older adults serve as honorary grandparents who visit classrooms, share stories, and give love.

Shrinking World

Communication technology and international travel have made the whole world as accessible as neighboring states were only a few years ago. We are closer to becoming a single global society.

The world is interdependent. National destiny is dependent on international banks, trade, and markets. No nation can stand alone. The business enterprise is targeted not only to local or national markets, but also to global markets. Many manufactured goods consist of parts made in many countries.

Once again, "change" is the operative word. The economic influence has shifted from West to East. The language and ethnic origin of people in the United States are changing. Immigration—a global immigration—is the source of population growth in the United States. Ethnic, national, and linguistic diversity is becoming evident in more and more cities and towns across the country. Included among the names of recent immigrants are Kim, Lee, Gonzalez, Lopez, and Persaud. Many have little understanding or contact with the Christian faith. The globalized population makes us all world citizens. The Christian church is now global and ministers in a context of global urbanization, with people moving to cities worldwide as never before. Issues increasingly are transcending national boundaries. Global warming, the destruction of the rain forest, ocean dumping, and acid rain are only a few of the environmental issues that affect our planet and demand global solutions.

These changes affect the twenty-first century Lutheran school in multiple ways. For example, Lutheran schools need to make intentional efforts to serve immigrant families. Many of these families have their initial contact with the church through the Lutheran school, which serves as the bridge. There is an increased need for Lutheran school teachers to have skills in cross-cultural relationships and communication. Lutheran schools are an obvious resource for language instruction. Students in Lutheran schools will reflect the growing pluralism in language, culture, and religious background. Lutheran schools will help congregation members and equip students to understand and appreciate people of various cultures, ethnic groups, and races. Those enrolled in Lutheran schools will be provided with the skills needed for successful living in a global society. Lutheran schools can make a major contribution to mission work in the cities by offering a unique doorway to the thousands of people who lack any connection to the church, but who seek the ministry of the school. Through the school they can be introduced to the total ministry of the church.

CHANGING VALUES

Our society provides a veritable supermarket of values and lifestyles. Globalization and secularization challenge the existence of any moral standard. The common fabric required for a democracy may be in jeopardy in a nation that has a culture that cannot agree on a set of values.

The trend in values focuses on self and self-fulfillment. It appears that many in our society possess unlimited desires in an age of limited resources. The world's resources are incapable of sustaining the growing world population at the level of consumption enjoyed in the United States today.

The television producer parents many children. Children will spend more hours watching television before graduation from high school than they will spend in any other activity except sleeping. The dominant narrative of television and television commercials is that we are what we own. How much of the radical change in culture brought about for fun and profit and the shifts in acceptable public behavior can be attributed to the crass values of the messenger of this narrative, i.e., the advertising industry, is, of course, arguable. However, money, luxury, and sanitized sex appear to be the values and powerful images thrown at children daily, telling them what it is to be human and contributing to the destruction of healthy family values. In addition to television, music videos and recordings compete with the Lutheran school for the attention of its students, often conveying a nihilistic message. The use of multimedia communication (sound, music, and visual) attracts today's young people.

The growth of various religions and the increasing interest in non-Christian spirituality, of which the New Age movement is but one example, challenge Lutheran schools. There is also growth in attitudes devaluing human life. Abortion, terrorism, doctor-assisted death, drive-by shootings, an increased suicide rate among youth, and increased child and spousal abuse all reflect the devaluing of human life in our society. The young and the healthy have become the new elite class.

Drugs and violence seem to permeate our society. Drugs and drug-related crimes have cast a widening pall over society. Violent criminals influence all areas of urban, suburban, and rural America. Children may have a different attitude toward war. The wars they know are short, high tech, and on television. They may perceive war as something like a game of Nintendo.

American society has moved from a churched to an unchurched mentality. We live in a post-Christian era. At best, contemporary society appears only to tolerate the church. Some can and do argue that our culture trivializes religion.[2] Many segments of society are seemingly antagonistic towards the church.

These changing values present an overwhelming challenge to Lutheran schools and teachers. With the passing of time, the values of the Lutheran school will probably stand in increasingly greater conflict with the values of our society in general. While the United States has a Judeo-Christian heritage, it is not a Christian country. Every Lutheran school is a mission station and every Lutheran teacher a missionary. New communication vehicles will be required in our classrooms. Students enrolled in Lutheran schools cannot be expected to hate rock and love Bach. All the arts must be used as means for conveying the Gospel in classrooms. Ultimately, Lutheran schools will have to encourage and equip students to become involved and engaged in moral and ethical discussions and decisions. Lutheran teachers must help their students understand that they are both private and public persons. To this end, Lutheran schools will continue to stress the private, e.g., personal salvation, but will also contribute increasingly to the creation of a public mind in their charges.

Changing Technology

Just as children today consider television to be a taken-for-granted necessity of life, children of tomorrow will take for granted the household computer. Yet, much of the technology children will use in this new millennium is still to be invented.

Technology continues to change. In the future, the telephone, computer, and television may be combined into one tool.

Information technology has increased the ability to develop, store, and retrieve vast amounts of information in a short period of time. While information technology is helpful, it is of no real value unless applied in some way to a useful purpose. Application of information is a growing, vital industry.

The increase in technology has caused vast savings in labor, but at the cost of jobs. Technology has brought higher expectations of quality and cost. Some people have begun to believe that all current problems can and will be solved by technology and information or that every possibility will be realized if one is patient enough. As Neil Postman, somewhat tongue in cheek, asserts,

---

[2] See Stephen L. Carter, *The Culture of Disbelief: How American Law and Politics Trivialize Religious Devotion* (New York: Anchor Books, 1993).

it becomes far from asinine to speak of the god of Technology—in the sense that people believe technology works, that they rely on it, that it makes promises, that they are bereft when denied access to it, that they are delighted when they are in its presence, that for most people it works in mysterious ways, that they condemn people who speak against it, that they stand in awe of it, and that, in the born-again mode, they will alter their lifestyles, their schedules, their habits, and their relationships to accommodate it. If this not be a form of religious belief, what is?[3]

God or not, communications technology (voice mail, beepers, cellular phones, laptop computers, etc.) is blurring the line between work and leisure. Increasingly, the workplace is traveling with the person.

Technology has become the fourth "R" of schooling at the dawn of the twenty-first century. People skilled in information technology will be important to the future ministry of the Lutheran school. Knowledge and skill in educational technology, especially in the use of computers, are regarded as so essential to Lutheran teachers that mastery of these resources is required in many synodical teacher-education programs. Technology will help the Lutheran school manage its ministry and increase its effectiveness.

As this new millennium begins, computers and computer-assisted instruction, the Internet, the World Wide Web, and CD-ROMs are increasingly becoming important additions to the Lutheran school classroom, changing the way teachers teach and students learn. They provide teachers and students in Lutheran schools with up-to-date information. They represent a new technological dynamic, building on such earlier breakthroughs as writing and the printing press, that dramatically increases the storage of information in readily accessible form.

Visual communication and advanced technology will assist the Lutheran school in fulfilling its mission. Lutheran high schools may become centers for developing artistic talent and the production skill necessary for sharing the Gospel in new, creative ways that combine hearing and seeing. Might Lutheran schools increase the church's influence in the arts and the entertainment field through the future performers and producers that pass through their doors? Through the Lutheran school, perhaps the church may even recapture its influence in the creative arts.

Unfortunately, however, technology decreases the necessity for personal, human contact. Thus, Lutheran schools must be balanced with "high touch" ministry. Lutheran teachers will need to remember that the Gospel enables and persuades Christ's people to provide support and care in a personal fellowship community.

---

[3] Neil Postman, *The End of Education: Redefining the Value of School* (New York: Alfred A. Knopf, 1995), 38.

The cost of acquiring and maintaining the new technology, which will require constant "updates" of hardware as well as software, will increase the cost of education in Lutheran schools. More than likely, it will also decrease the amount of congregational funds to support school ministry.

Changing Education

While few people attended high school in the 1890s, there were jobs on farms, as well as in businesses and factories, where a high school education was not required. Today, limited employment opportunities are available for those without a high school diploma.

Quality, world-class education is necessary for our country and our congregations. We cannot compete as a nation without quality education. Yet, rightly or wrongly, there is a perception, especially as it relates to urban areas, that the quality of education is declining.

Today most education in America occurs in schools where a person's education is judged not by the amount of knowledge they have, but by the number of years they have attended school or by the number of degrees and certificates they have accumulated. In the future, education will not be limited by classroom walls. Learning will continue throughout life and through information technology, formal schooling, training centers, and informal networks.

Schooling for all ages through electronic networks will be common. Learning will be more self-directed and will be developmentally appropriate for each learner. Education for children and adults will occur simultaneously—and at times in the same place as parents, grandparents, and children attend school or use personal computers at home at the same time.

Because many corporations do not believe that schools are providing sufficient basic skills in math and reading, they will step up their intervention in the education process because they believe that this will be necessary in order to insure that they will have an adequately prepared workforce. The role and financial investment of private industry in employee education and retraining will continue to grow.

Educators, especially in urban public schools, will continue to face major challenges in accomplishing their task because of the increasingly heavy social baggage carried into schools by children, the limited financial resources from which they can draw, entrenched bureaucracy, political in-fighting, and, perhaps most importantly, the loss of a common standard of community values. The cost of education at all levels will continue to increase rapidly.

Driven in part by the perception that competition will improve education, the parental-choice movement in public, private, and parochial schools will continue to grow. If Lutheran schools are not included, will they not be at a severe disadvantage?

Due in part to parental choice, there will be increased governmental interest in and regulation of non-public schools. This may occur especially where non-public schools make up a large portion of a community's educational institutions.

There will be a shortage of good teachers. Many will work at a higher wage, training corporate employees. Others will work in corporate child-care centers or corporate-sponsored schools.

Schools are and will continue to be major social service institutions. Schools provide not only education, but also child care full-time and before and after classes, two or three meals a day, counseling services, and parent social groups. The recent growth of child care by Lutheran schools may be attributed to their traditional emphasis on the cooperation among home, church, and school.

The growth of child care and early childhood centers as a part of Lutheran elementary and secondary schools is changing the scope and style of these schools. The growth of child care and early childhood centers in congregations without elementary schools is leading many within the Missouri Synod to modify their concept of "school" and "teacher."

One implication of the aforementioned educational changes is that the changing nature of Lutheran schools must be affirmed. They are not only a major part of the Synod's ministry, but they are recognized and valued in many communities and nationally. They will need to continue to be advocates for the education of the total person, including the spiritual aspect, as people seek not only education but also significance in life. More than likely, a substantial number of Lutheran school leaders will continue to speak out aggressively in support of parental choice in education. There will be fewer synodically certified teachers available for ministry in Lutheran schools because of lower numbers in synodical universities preparing persons for the teaching ministry. The number of female administrators will continue to increase as we begin our journey through the new millennium, continuing a trend that began in the 1980s.

THE VILLAGE AND THE CAMP REVISITED

Lutheran schools have an important role in the future ministry of the church. The mission of the school will become ever more vital as we continue to nurture our children and reach out with the hope of the Gospel, but the challenges to maintain the schools will also increase.

Lutheran schools in this new millennium will operate year-around. Adults and children may be in school or learning elsewhere at the same time. Lifelong learning will be a must. The need for mentoring will increase as information multiplies. Distance learning by computer networks and teleconferences will expand the scope of educational resources and teaching personnel and allow for mentoring relationships through various networks. All education will have spiritual overtones as people seek significance or meaning in life, not just information.

The Lutheran school has existed in our country for more than a century as an extension of the congregation to nurture the faith of its students. For decades the congregation has been the source of students, leadership, and money. Today the school provides an agency through which the church can touch the world. Lutheran schools on all levels serve many people who have no previous contact with the church or with the Gospel. The school is the door to the church's ministry for many children and adults.

When we were a village church, there was no need to connect with the world. A village was a closed system. But now we need this connection. In many cases a reverse in flow will take place. Churches that once supported a school will be supported in part by the school. Instead of the congregation providing students for the school, the school will provide members for the congregation. The changing nature of Lutheran schools can be seen by looking at those served by and serving in this ministry. Viewing these groups on the basis of our changing world helps us see the changes.

STUDENTS

In the village the child went to school at about age five. Today many children have attended school or child care for two or more years before the age of five. In the Lutheran schools of the past students were Lutheran, white, English-speaking, achievement directed, and concerned about getting a good education and the eventual diploma. There was a common set of expectations among students and the school.

From the camp viewpoint, we see students from various cultural and racial backgrounds, a growing number of those whose language at home is not English. They come from a variety of Christian backgrounds, and some are members of non-Christian churches. An increasing number are unchurched. Some have high social service needs and some lag in social skills. Students and their parents are seeking schools where those served by them have an identity, are valued, and are safe.

PARENTS

In the village, parents were active members of the congregation supporting the school. They viewed the Lutheran school as an extension of their family and placed high value on Christian education. The values taught in Lutheran schools were reinforced at home. Parents were white and spoke English or German as their native language.

On the other hand, parents from the camp represent a diverse mix of ethnic and racial groups. They are consumer oriented. They have a variety of high expectations of the school. They want a school that is physically safe. They want a school where they can trust the teachers. They send their children to school for a quality education and moral training, though their values may differ significantly from the values taught in the Lutheran school. Their spirituality is often undeveloped. Many will sacrifice or work a second job for their children to attend a Lutheran school.

TEACHERS AND STAFF

In the village the school teachers were graduates of a synodical teacher-education program. The teachers, both male and female, responded to the call to the teaching ministry and served in a very predictable context, similar to their own religious and ethnic backgrounds. A majority of the teachers, even in the lower elementary grades, were male. All school administrators were male. The administrator was part-time, and his tasks were very predictable. Teachers were held in high regard by the congregation. The teaching ministry was viewed as essential to the ministry of the church.

In the camp, teachers have a variety of backgrounds. Some are members of The Lutheran Church—Missouri Synod, some are members of other Lutheran bodies, and most of the others come from various Christian backgrounds. A few are not members of Christian churches. The declining number of synodical teacher graduates of various cultures limits the opportunities of congregations to call synodically-certified teachers.

Teachers will need continuing staff development to meet new curriculum standards. There will be the need for more specialists in computers and foreign-language instruction. Teaching the faith will require new strategies. The complexity of the camp school will require that schools have full-time administrators. The school secretary has a key role in the camp school, since the secretary often is the first contact with parents and other citizens of the community. As the school responds to the needs of the students, parents, and communities they serve, the role of the Lutheran teacher and administrator will expand. In addressing those needs, Lutheran teaching ministers will assume such offices as counselor, social worker, and social service personnel much more than they did in the village. Increasingly, the role of the twenty-first century Lutheran teacher will be that of surrogate parent.

CONGREGATIONS

In the village the pastor is the key leader of the school. The school is an important part of the ministry of the congregation. The congregation has a school to nurture its children who are baptized in the faith. The school is a source of pride and status for the congregation. The majority of students in the school are from the congregation, so there is a mutually interdependent relationship.

In the camp the role of the pastor may seem unclear. Pastors are trained in a village mentality of predictability and control. The role of the pastor changes as the enrollment in the school has a greater percentage of nonmembers who have a limited relationship with the pastor. The attitude of the congregation toward unchurched or other-churched parents influences their willingness to affiliate with the congregation. The congregation may view the school as a mission, i.e., a place where the Gospel is shared; as evangelism, i.e., an opportunity for a personal compelling witness to Jesus Christ; or as membership recruitment, i.e., developing strategies to have parents become part of the worshiping fellowship.

The school may be the new place where the church interfaces with the world. The number of children the congregation baptizes each year will determine if the school is to focus on nurture or nurture and mission. The financial resources of the congregation available to the school will depend on the vision of the school and the number of children attending from the congregation. As tuition from nonmembers underwrites a greater share of the total cost, efforts must be made to maintain a ministry perspective of the school.

Community

The community values quality education because it produces good citizens. In many communities, the Lutheran school is a welcome addition, although some communities see the Lutheran school as competing with the public schools for students and money.

The changing role of a Lutheran school provides for new opportunities to serve the community. The Lutheran school helps to maintain community stability by offering quality Christian education. The Lutheran school can serve as a model of quality education in a safe environment and give credibility to the witness of the church.

Lutheran educators will need to address, cautiously to be sure, the new opportunities that may emerge for our schools to link up with businesses looking for quality workers who have mastered the basic skills. Lutheran schools are likely to play an increasingly important role in our pluralistic society, as a greater variety of values and religious teaching enter society's mainstream. There seems to be a growing positive attitude by the public toward the Lutheran school.

The Lord of the Church

Finally, but of first importance, is the Lord of the church. In the village the school was viewed as an agency to nurture those already in the flock. It was an extension of the role of family in the spiritual development of the child. In the camp the school has a mission focus. While nurturing the faith remains an important task, the school develops spiritual awakening through the working of the Holy Spirit as God's Word is taught.

In addition, the Lutheran school provides formation of the faith and the development of the spiritual and devotional life. Preparing students for ministry, not just teaching "religion," expands the role of the school. Experimental instruction in spirituality and the open sharing of faith will lead to an emphasis on right behavior as well as right answers. Lutheran schools serve the Lord as his mission to the world, not just to the church. Lutheran school teachers provide the compassion of Christ and lead others to be compassionate in Christ's name. They model their lifestyle as committed Christians.

The journey for those about to enter the Lutheran teaching ministry will be challenging. The future sometimes seems so overwhelming or threatening that some of you may want to delay the journey or turn back. For others of you the journey presents new opportunities and stimulates new solutions. There are no easy answers for those of us who travel on this journey of faith.

However, in Jesus we have strength and power. Christ gives us more than we ask or imagine. His power in us is the same power that God used when he raised Christ from the dead—resurrection power!

Summing Up

This chapter was intended to be more than a trip through time. It is to be hoped that it provided those readers who are about to enter the teaching ministry of The Lutheran Church—Missouri Synod with a new understanding of the scope and style of Lutheran schools as they embark on ministry in this new millennium. Since we have not traveled this path before, the trip should generate excitement and the prospects of new challenges and possibilities for ministry.

Discussion Topics and Suggested Projects

1. How might the trend away from the village and toward the camp affect your future ministry as a Lutheran teacher?

2. Provide specific examples of how Lutheran schools can assist families of the types listed in the chapter.

3. In addition to the suggestions in this chapter, how else might a Lutheran school use the talents of older adults?

4. What signs do you see that indicate that you live in a global community?

5. What will enhance or hinder the Lutheran school's role in shaping values?

6. Why might some veteran Lutheran teachers who have lived through such highly touted cure-alls as 16-millimeter film, closed circuit television, 8-millimeter film, teacher-proof texts, and now computers, to name a few, be skeptical of the "god of Technology"?

7. How might the Lutheran school that you serve use changing technology in
   - school administration?
   - the instructional process?
   - communicating the school's mission and ministry?

8. What might be the downside of parental choice for Lutheran schools?

9. What aspects of the village, if any, would you argue for the Lutheran school to maintain in this new millennium?

RESOURCES, INFLUENCES, AND SUGGESTED FURTHER READING

Barker, Joel A. *Discovering the Future: The Business of Paradigms*. 2nd ed. Burnsville, Minn.: Charthouse Learning Corporation, 1988. Videocassette.

Barker, Joel A. *Discovering the Future: The Business of Paradigms*. 2nd ed. St. Paul: ILI Press, 1988.

Callahan, Kennon L. *Effective Church Leadership: Building on the Twelve Keys*. San Francisco: Harper Row, 1990.

Carter, Stephen L. *The Culture of Disbelief: How American Law and Politics Trivialize Religious Devotion*. New York: Anchor Books, 1993.

Cornish, Edward. "The Cyber Future: 92 Ways Our Lives Will Change By the Year 2025." *The Futurist* 30 (January–February 1996): 1–15.

Dunn, Samuel. "Christianity's Future: The First-World Church Takes a Back Seat." *The Futurist* 23 (March–April 1989): 34–37.

George, Carl. *Prepare Your Church for the Future*. Tarrytown, N.Y.: Revell Company, 1991.

Luecke, David. *Evangelical Style and Lutheran Substance: Facing America's Mission Challenge*. St. Louis: Concordia Publishing House, 1988.

Michael, Donald N. *The Unprepared Society: Planning for a Precarious Future*. New York: Harper Colophon, 1968.

Moser, Carl J. "The Changing Lutheran School." *Lutheran Education* 124 (March–April 1989): 205–211.

Postman, Neil. *The End of Education: Redefining the Value of School*. New York: Alfred A. Knopf, 1995.

Rietschel, William C. "The Crisis of Democratic Authority and the Ends of Lutheran Education." *Lutheran Education* 134 (September–October 1998): 18–26.

Schaef, Anne Wilson, and Diane Fassel. *The Addictive Organization*. San Francisco: Harper Row, 1988.

Schaller, Lyle E. *It's a Different World: The Challenge for Today's Pastor*. Nashville: Abingdon Press, 1987.

U.S. Census Bureau. "Projection of the Population of States by Age and Race: 1988–2080." Washington, D.C., 1988.

Weems, Lovett H., Jr. *Church Leadership: Vision, Team, Culture and Integrity*. Nashville: Abingdon Press, 1993.

Weiner, Edith, and Arnold Brown. "Human Factor: The Gap Between Humans and Machines." *The Futurist* 23 (May–June 1989): 9–11.

Yankelovich, Daniel. *New Rules in American Life: Searching for Self-Fulfillment in a World Turned Upside Down*. New York: Random House, 1981.